FROM THE BACK OF THE HOUSE

Memoir of a Broadway Theatre Manager

Dan Landon

IBiS
BOOKS

Book Cover by 100Covers

First edition 2024

ISBN-13: 978-1-956672-23-7 (Paperback edition)

ISBN-13: 978-1-956672-24-4 (Ebook edition)

Contents

They're only words... unless they're true.

David Mamet

Prologue

IF YOU ARE HOLDING this book, I would assume we have something between us that is fantastic: a love of the wonderful art form of theatre. A love of it from the Off-Off-Broadway lofts with leaking ceiling pipes in downtown Manhattan, to Community theatres, to Regional, to Off-Broadway, to Broadway itself.

The lights go down and come up again and we are willing, longing, to be transported to another world, or the most realistic depiction of this world we could imagine. We know it's good if it speaks to us, and we say that's true.

We might know or have seen each other before because, for over 9000 performances, I was at the back of the house of the Broadway theatres you may have attended over the last 40 years.

I was the "house" manager on those shows, although I much preferred the term "theatre manager," because I was responsible for everything within and often outside the theatre. Even the water in Alec Baldwin's dressing room was my concern.

I first dreamed of being an actor, and I was, but emotionally I couldn't wait for the phone to ring soon after a big audition. Was I neurotic? To call an actor neurotic is redundant! But that was me, and I was not emotionally suited to the constant rejection, the waiting and not knowing that is a young actor's life.

But eventually I found a way to remain in the most collaborative of art forms, and I know how a show gets put together more than most. If you ever wanted to know about that, or what happens after Opening Night has come and gone, then go with me on my journey through fifty shows and my many encounters with the famous and great of the theatre, their frailties and courage, as they pursue their "craft, or sullen art."

These words and stories are true, and remembered.

***

Broadway.

A definition more than a word. A place that thousands upon thousands of young actors dream about.

Older actors fondly remember their days on Broadway, if they were good enough—and this is important—lucky enough, to have been *"walking the boards"* in one show, or ten.

For those of us who work on and around the glittering lights of Times Square, as I did for thirty-seven years, the neighborhood was like a studio lot. I would run into five people I had worked with on various shows in the distance of two blocks.

The people of the theatre are usually kind as they ask what show you are working on, and how it is doing.

As my old boss Gerry Schoenfeld, Chairman of the Shubert Organization, used to say, "Everyone wants to be associated with a hit. That's the happy time."

How right he was.

There is a world of people, those who do not act or sing, direct or write, who nevertheless labor in the Broadway theatre, sometimes for decades. The stagehands, ushers, treasurers (the people in the box office), musicians, stage managers, porters, stage doormen, company and theatre (house) managers. That's what I was, the manager of the theatre.

Fiercely loyal to the "buildings" (theatres) that we work in, all of us depend also upon the shows that run in them. If the show closes and the theatre goes dark, after we take out the scenery and lights, our work ends until another show books the theatre and the lights of the marquee glow again.

There was never an opening night I was not thrilled and brimming with hope for that show.

There was never a closing I would not gaze at the empty stage in the semi-darkness, and think of the incredible fleeting nature of theatre, and the illusion of life we present.

Fifty shows. I was so lucky, as I said. This is the story of those shows and how Broadway and the world of New York itself changed. In the end, it is only the single ghost light on stage. But, on the way it is the emotion, the funny memories, the fondly recalled ovations, the audience lingering in a special place with the curtain down, the stage lights dimmed, the story told.

In the expanse of my career, I saw the show *Da*, with Bernard Hughes and Brian Murray, play a Broadway theatre, the Morosco, in 1978. It was produced for $125,000.

In 2015, a revival of *The Front Page*, with stars Nathan Lane and John Goodman, was produced at the Broadhurst, another Broadway house, for a budget of $4,000,000.

What happened?

Here's the lowdown from one Broadway insider.

ACT ONE

The Bad Old, Good Old Days

Whoopi

SHE WAS UNKNOWN. WITHIN three years, she would be a household name. Her name was Whoopi.

The renowned stage and screen director Mike Nichols wanted to present a new comic he had spotted in a downtown club in a one-person show. The question was, "Who—or even what—was a Whoopi Goldberg?"

No one knew. Everyone was convinced even the great Mike Nichols wouldn't be able to breathe life into her career, which was a tad ironic because Whoopi had been a cosmetician in a mortuary. But it soon happened that there was no stopping this young, hip, black woman from the West Coast.

I remember the first morning Mike pulled up to the theatre in an outrageously expensive black Mercedes. I told his driver it was a beautiful car.

"He has three of them just like that," he said. Mike walked inside the theatre and eyeballed me.

"Who are you?" he asked.

"I'm the manager of the theatre," I said.

"Are you out of high school?" Mike replied.

I said nothing. But the message was loud and clear: there was an eight-hundred-pound gorilla in the room.

During rehearsal, a middle-aged black woman came to the stage door.

"I'm Whoopi's cousin. I want to see her."

"We're on a break. But she should be back in a minute," I said.

"I'll just sit and wait for her."

A minute later, Whoopi strolled in and shook her head. As she walked past me, she whispered, "She's not my cousin!"

Fame, or in this case, sudden fame, can be a bitch. Or, as Whoopi was fond of saying in those days, "Life's a bitch, and then you die."

With the miracle of Mike Nichols seeing her comedy act downtown, and saying to her, "I'll present you and your characters anywhere, even Broadway," a supreme confidence had entered her.

Yes, she was good. Yes, she was funny. Her talent had landed, and it was even bigger than the size of Mike's car. We invited a guest audience to the Lyceum to see this rising star in a first dress rehearsal. Whoopi walked onstage, with long, luxurious dreadlocks, and she proceeded to present almost three-and-a-half hours of her comedic characters.

Most of it was brilliant, but by the second act, the audience had started to squirm. Mike's magic as a director was greatly needed. He cut the set down to less than two hours, with six of Whoopi's different characters making up the show. We got good reviews, but the public did not come.

The opening night was filled with stars, made up of all of Mike Nichols' friends he had directed in movies. I overheard a wide-eyed waitress at the first-night party ask *The Chinatown* star, "Are you really Jack Nicholson?"

Jack, behind sunglasses, nodded in that famous style.

"Yeah."

Celebrities galore came to every performance. I took the rock star Sting backstage and thought, as a full-blooded heterosexual, that he was the most handsome man I had ever seen. One night, even Steven Spielberg came by. After the show, with the audience gone, he stood center stage talking with Whoopi.

About seven anxious paparazzi stood in the lobby like wild animals in a pen waiting for their chance to take a picture of the *Jaws* director. I had to hold them back. After twenty minutes, I went to lock up my office for the night and closed the outer lobby doors.

But when I came out of my office, the paparazzi had somehow gained access to the building and they were all next to the stage, snapping pictures of Whoopi and Spielberg. I figured they must've slipped in when one of the crew exited the building by the large wooden lobby doors.

The next day I got a call from the show's publicist saying that Spielberg was "angry as a wet cat" and thought it the height of being unprofessional.

He was threatening to call anyone at Shubert who would take his call.

I told my side of the story to Mike Nichols.

"How much trouble am I in?" I asked.

"Forget about it. He wants her for the lead role in a movie he's making based on Alice Walker's novel, *The Color Purple*. Now her agent, Sandy Gallin, knows it, and that will drive the price up."

In the early days when the show was struggling, the Company Manager, Max Allentuck, close to eighty, had a problem with all the money I was making because of union premiums.

We had an eleven o'clock show on Saturdays: that was a premium.

Three shows on that day: another premium.

Other rules forced other premiums.

Max was a legendary manager and the subject of several famous theatre stories. The foremost story told about Max was really about Maureen Stapleton, the legendary character actress, and Max's wife for a time. Maureen was playing Birdie in Lillian Hellman's *The Little Foxes* in Washington with Elizabeth Taylor.

Nancy Reagan, then the first lady of the country, came backstage and was properly greeted with total dignity by the cast.

Then she got to Maureen, who addressed her informally as Nancy, saying: "Hey, Nancy! How are you doing? How's Ronnie, Nancy?"

Lillian Hellman, who had been feuding with Maureen since the New York engagement of the play, approached Maureen and chided her, "How dare you address the first lady of this country in such a disrespectful manner!"

"Relax, Lillian. We go back a long time. Nancy had an affair with my second husband when I was still married to him," Maureen replied, referring to Mr. Allentuck.

Max was actually invited to the White House during the Reagan administration and had a private lunch with both Nancy and Ronnie.

One night, Manny Azenberg, legendary producer for Neil Simon, introduced me to Carl Reiner. "Max was the manager of my play *Enter Laughing*. They told me at the time Max was the only honest manager on Broadway."

Max retired in his eighties when he could no longer read the payroll. A thin man with a full head of grey hair, he once said in front of the whole box office, "Dan's salary is going to close the show."

And then a miracle happened about three months into the run when Manny Azenberg decided to make a television commercial promoting the show. Hallelujah! Ticket sales skyrocketed. We would go on to run for twenty weeks, only closing because exhaustion set in for Whoopi from having to do it eight times a week, twice on Friday, and three times on Saturday.

Also, it didn't help that Whoopi, even though she neither smoked nor drank, would love going out with the many celebrities who came to see her, hanging out late into the night.

Near the end of the run, Whoopi brought Warren Beatty, who was single at the time, into the theatre for a Sunday matinee, and they stood talking on stage. My crew of female ushers gazed at them. On leaving, Warren had to walk down the long hallway that led to 46th Street and out the stage door, and as he did so, Whoopi and the ushers stared at him until he left.

Then Whoopi pretended to faint dead away, and everyone burst out laughing. One of the younger girls yelled out to Whoopi, "Hey, Whoopi, do you share?"

Whoopi picked herself up, walked offstage to her dressing room, and said something very wise: "To share, you have to have."

Among the many celebrities who became Whoopi's fans was Andy Warhol. One night, the icon came by and gave Whoopi one of his famous "Marilyn Monroe" portraits.

We put it by the stage doorman to guard all night.

I said to John, my doorman, "Whatever you do, don't let the painting out of your sight for a second."

After the show, with visitors all around backstage, I saw the Warhol leaning against the wall and no doorman in sight. I was livid, to say the least. I waited with the painting until Whoopi left the Theatre with it safely in tow.

But the doorman was the least of my troubles. Mike Nichols was unhappy with my staff. He claimed they made too much noise as they sat latecomers. There were other problems.

"The bartenders are making too much noise putting ice in the drinks before intermission," Mike moaned.

Throughout my career, I was to learn that directors or producers could become very unhappy about the theatre crew when they felt unsure about their show.

Then, "It's too hot." Or, "There's noise coming from outside. Stop that jackhammer down the street!" And so on.

I had several meetings with the old and young Westside Irish ushers who worked for me to address these issues.

But Mike's complaints continued until it reached the point that he was going to go above my head to Gerry Schoenfeld, which would have been bad for me.

The head usher, Marion Fleming, a very attractive woman in her early fifties, stopped Mike one night and in a stern manner told him: "You know, Mr. Nichols, I love Whoopi, too. You're not the only one. We want the patrons to be quiet too, and we're doing the best job we can."

"It stunned me," Mike confessed to me some thirty years later. Someone other than himself actually cared about the show?

Manny Azenberg told me, "Please go and meet Mike at the stage door, and walk with him after a matinee. Listen to what he wants."

Again!

I did so with great trepidation as we walked toward Broadway.

"The ushers still have to be quieter seating latecomers," he said.

"I've told them that. I'll tell them again."

"Make sure the concession kids remember they're in a theatre and not pouring drinks at Studio 54."

"I will. They're all young actors. They should know."

Finally, we approached Broadway where the new Marriott Hotel was being built huge and foreboding. We both paused and looked up at it, standing there in silence.

"Look at that thing! That will be the kind of place you can take three call girls into at once, and not get noticed," Mike said.

Whoopi soon told Manny Azenberg that she couldn't go on due to exhaustion. But at that point, the show had recouped, paid back the original investment, and all was well.

It was around this time that we heard word that Lorne Michaels of Saturday Night Live wanted to produce a videotape of the evening through his company, Broadway Video.

Manny asked me if I would like to general manage the taping. I was thrilled, but then I learned there was a catch. Lorne did not want to pay the fee that Mike's agent Sam Cohn had requested for him to direct the television presentation. He had hired a very good television director named Tommy Schlamme.

However, that meant that Mike was going to have to watch someone else direct his show. It did not, however, mean that Mike would not be around every minute of the recording seething with sarcasm. At the height of the shoot, I was running around like crazy, and I passed Mike and he said to me, "Well, I see no job is too small."

It was the best-selling comedy video recording in the country the next year and Whoopi won a Grammy for it. It was a rare smash hit for the Lyceum Theatre in those days.

That fall, I was assigned to the Longacre Theatre on 48th Street on the "right side" of Broadway (that would be the west side), as the musical chairs of Shubert managers spun.

During the run of Whoopi's show, I took the great rock and blues singer Patti LaBelle backstage. I asked her about a lyric in her hit song *Lady Marmalade*. What did the lyric *gitchi, gitchi, ya, ya da da da, gitchi your ya ya here* mean?

Ms. LaBelle, straight-faced and ever the lady, said, "I don't know. I never knew."

It sums up the truth about a Broadway show: you never know if it's going to be a hit or not. It's all in the hands of the gods.

The Bad Old Days

To understand the world of New York that Whoopi played in on 45th Street, we must go back in time to when I was first assigned to Broadway's oldest theatre, the Lyceum, after my time as an apprentice manager was over.

In the early 80s, to walk down 42nd Street was to witness an unsavory sight. There was an endless string of porn shops, drug dealers, and stairways off the street that led to seedy houses of prostitution. They were all places you were more likely to be robbed and stabbed than anything else.

The old theatres along the street that once held Broadway shows in the 30s and 40s were now the home of porno and violent exploitation films.

I recall walking down the street locally known as *The Deuce*—there was later a TV series made about its grittiness, starring James Franco—one night when a young man, no more than twenty, turned around and fired a shot with a .22 caliber pistol. It could have been a deal gone bad, or an evil look, or one of a hundred bad excuses for attempted murder.

One steamy summer night, from my apartment window at Manhattan Plaza, I saw a man stumble out of the SRO Hotel across the street, only to crumble in the gutter, hurt and bleeding. I'll never forget the haunting image of the police squad car lights spinning in front of the crime scene late into the night until his body was covered with a sheet and taken away.

I found myself wondering who would live here in ten years? Most importantly, who in their right mind would go to the theatre if the streets remained this way?

The Lyceum was built "uptown" in 1903 by Daniel Frohman, when most of the other theatres were on 14th Street.

A beautiful theatre, but when I arrived to take over, it was badly in need of renovation, with its frayed seats and ancient carpets.

On the corner near 6th Avenue, there was a rundown hotel out of which pimps and street walking prostitutes plied their trade late into the Times Square night. One of my jobs as the manager when we opened with a show about every four or five months was to politely ask the girls not to stand directly under the marquee, which they did with impunity when the theatre was dark.

Thankfully, most of them were understanding about this and didn't want to draw the type of heat that such a confrontation with the theatre would bring. However, one of the working girls saw opportunity.

The lobby doors were now open so the box office could sell tickets. My then head treasurer, Rob Bauer, told me that one of these girls was taking clients up the stairs to this small area next to the heavy wooden doors which lead to the seats of the mezzanine.

These doors were locked when there was no performance, but the foyer itself could be used to do the deed out of the sight.

I took to coming in early during daytime hours in an effort to catch her and, sure enough, on the very second day of my stakeout she came—no pun intended—in with a guy in a UPS uniform!

I ran up the stairs and shouted, "What are you doing up here?"

The UPS man ran down the stairs, fumbling at his belt as he dashed out of the lobby. The girl, however, seemed unfazed. Cool as can be, she slowly descended the marble stairs with its brass handrail.

I stopped her and said, "Wait a second. I want to talk to you. If I catch you up here again doing your thing, I'm going down to that hotel on the corner and tell them what you're doing. Namely, cutting them out of their share."

Still cool, she continued to stare at me.

I added, "You know what that'll mean, then?"

I obviously did not want that to happen. The look in her eyes changed.

"Don't worry," she said as she walked back out onto 45th Street, and she never came back.

***

The first big attraction in the Lyceum when I started there was *Master Harold and the Boys* written by the brilliant South African playwright Athol Fugard. The play, which starred Lonny Price, was about a young man's treatment in South Africa of his two black servants, played by Danny Glover and Zakes Mokae, a South African actor who had actually lived under apartheid.

Early in the run, three young boys wandered into the crowded lobby just before we opened the doors to the theatre. I warily kept an eye on them, which wasn't hard because they stuck out like a sore thumb amid the matinee ladies.

Then they suddenly struck, ripping the pocketbook off of the shoulder of an old woman and running like mad out of the lobby. What angered me most was the last of the three saluted me before he ran out, knowing I must be the manager.

As fate would have it, the second time they came back, Danny Glover was standing next to me as the audience entered. There is an unwritten law that the audience doesn't see members of the cast before the curtain goes up, but Danny was new to all this. His great appeal as an actor was this naturalness. He was a proud man who had known the streets.

I started yelling, as I knew what these three boys were up to: "Ladies and Gentlemen, please watch your pocketbooks and wallets!"

But it did not deter them. One of them again grabbed an old woman's pocketbook and ran out the large oak wooden doors with his friends. Danny, all six foot three and two hundred thirty pounds of him, ran after them. I took off close behind, being no less a scrapper in my day.

They ran toward Broadway. Before they were halfway there, Danny had clobbered one of them, tackling him to the ground. Another boy, the one who had ripped the pocketbook off my patron's shoulder, held it up so we could see it and then dropped it to the ground.

I was about to sprint after them when Danny grabbed my arm.

"We got it back. That's enough," he reasoned.

We returned to the lobby, with Danny holding the pocketbook up to tumultuous applause. We were heroes for a moment, no matter how foolish.

During another matinee, after the show had started, there was a knock on my office door. It was the chief usher Marion Fleming. "Mr. Landon, a lady has fallen."

She had tripped over this guy sleeping at the back of the house. I went out into the dark house and looked down. It was the playwright Athol Fugard! He had passed out drunk against the back wall of the orchestra shortly after the start of the first act.

We easily picked the small Athol up and helped him out to the lobby, sitting him on a chair. We called the producer Manny Azenberg. By this time he was a man known by all in the world of theatre for his work with Neil Simon. But years earlier, he had been denied entrance several times into the union ATPAM (Association of Theatrical Press Agents and Managers) by Secretary-Treasurer Dick Weaver. Manny finally had the chutzpah to go up to Weaver's office with his children and ask him: "How am I going to support them if you won't let me in this union?"

Soon after, Simon and his original producer, Saint Subber, decided to part ways. Neil then said to Manny, his company manager on his current show: "Why don't you produce my shows?"

It quickly led to one of the great managerial careers in the history of Broadway. I had heard Manny called a "Mensch"—meaning a real man, a good guy—on countless occasions by other people of the theatre.

Along with another producer of the show, named Jim Freydberg, they got Athol into treatment for his alcoholism. Athol eventually became sober and a long-distance runner. As of writing, he is full of vim and vigor, with only a few short years to get to his ninetieth birthday.

The sorrow he witnessed in South Africa, with the belittlement and oppression of black people, echoes in every line of his many poignant and uplifting plays. But that afternoon he was the drunken, passed-out playwright, whose own patron had tripped over him. The world of Manhattan and Times Square was this with its almost hourly robberies, street hustling, and prostitution.

That world of the mid-80s had to change in order for Broadway to survive.

There was great controversy at the time concerning the building of a grand forty-eight-story hotel on the block along Broadway between 45th and 46th Street. John Portman had first submitted his plans in the early 1970s, but the fiscal crisis and other things delayed the start of the project until ten years later.

Schoenfeld and Jacobs, the heads of Shubert, were in favor of the project even though it required the demolition of three small Broadway playhouses: the Helen Hayes, the little Bijou, and the Morosco where the play *Da* by Hugh Leonard had played.

There was enormous opposition in the theatre community. Superman himself, Christopher Reeve, Susan Sarandon, Colleen Dewhurst, and Joseph Papp stood in line with hundreds of actors who opposed the destruction of these theatrical gems for the construction of a behemoth hotel.

But Schoenfeld and Jacobs recognized there was a war on, and that the only way to take back Times Square from the criminal element was through the large investment of companies like Mr. Portman's and the Marriott chain.

They believed that the only way to revitalize Times Square was through legitimate businesses, not involved in pornography, and all the other unsavory things that made the area unfriendly to tourists, whether they were from Long Island or Iowa or London.

People ridiculed Jacobs and Schoenfeld, saying that it wasn't one of their theatres that had to come down. I remember Schoenfeld addressing a class one day in the Lyceum after a matinee about how hard it was to book a theatre like the one they were sitting in on the "wrong" side of Broadway (and that would be the east side).

For even when vacant, the city taxes, the insurance, and the energy costs remain the same. The fight to save the three playhouses was taken all the way up to the New York Supreme Court, where the developer won out. One of the last protests occurred in front of the theatres where Mr. Papp announced that anyone wishing to be arrested needed to stand in the parking lot next to the old theatres.

A hundred and seventy people volunteered and were taken away to be booked by the police. Then a backhoe with "Godzilla" written on the side went to work, much to lamentation by the remaining protesters.

The war would be won over many years as Times Square changed to be the safe environment for theatregoers that Schoenfeld and Jacobs desired. It required investment and legislation by the city that limited the location of topless clubs and porno shops.

The booming Times Square of today is the result.

***

The next attraction at the Lyceum was an Edward Albee play entitled *The Man Who had Three Arms*. During an early critics' performance (usually one of the performances in the week before the official opening), I was standing in the lobby with Mr. Albee.

At intermission, the first out of the theatre was Frank Rich, the critic of The New York Times. He had had thrown himself against the wooden doors at the back of the house, seeming, for all the world, to be having a terrible asthma attack.

I asked him if he needed help and all I could hear was his whisper, "... the play... the play."

That was what we call in the theatre a bad sign. Charlie Willard came around the corner into the lobby, wearing a cowboy hat, which was his trademark. Charlie was the company manager of *I Remember Mama*, my first Broadway Show.

Again, I had returned to stand right next to Mr Albee. Charlie must not have known who he was because he said loudly: "Boy, Dan, I hope you have another booking lined up."

I looked at Albee, who appeared to be unfazed. This was the man who had written *Zoo Story, A Delicate Balance, Who's Afraid of Virginia Woolf?*

So what did he need to prove, right?

We did no business, and the play closed in two weeks on April 17. It looked like I was in for a long layoff since there were no bookings on the horizon for the old Lyceum.

Then, something happened. Jack Yorke, the manager of the Majestic Theatre, where *42nd Street*, David Merrick's smash extravaganza was playing, suddenly took ill. I was asked to go there and fill in until Jack came back. If he came back. He was ninety-five years old.

He was legally deaf. His eyes were bad. He wore glasses, but he still did his huge payroll at the Majestic with great efficiency. Any problems with the audience were handled by veteran head ushers as if they were sergeants in the Army protecting the captain.

Jack had been a successful producer of such shows as *Brigadoon*, but his last show or two, it was rumored, had left him in debt to Shubert. One way they would let producers pay them back was by giving them a house (theatre) to work, the debt taken off through weekly deductions of their pay.

I was moved from the little Lyceum to the gigantic Majestic Theatre. I remembered seeing the show when it originated at the Winter Garden, a year or so before. My seat was very close to the stage, and when the curtain went up, the vibration of 50 dancers, tapping for all they were worth, could be felt on your chest. It was a throwback to the large grand old musicals of the past.

On the day of the show's opening, its director, Gower Champion, who had been ill, had died in the hospital. Merrick, ever the showman, abandoned good taste and announced at the curtain that Mr. Champion had passed away that day. The cast did not know, and reacted the way you would imagine, with howls of despair and grief.

Jerry Orbach, the show's star, started screaming: "Take the curtain down! Take it down!"

Mr. Merrick, always crazy as a fox, knew what he was doing. The publicity was legendary and the box office had lines around the block the next day. After a year, the show was moved from the Winter Garden to the Majestic.

It meant Andrew Lloyd Webber's hit from London, *Cats*, now had a house because the Winter Garden was big enough for that show, which required the making of a hole in the roof so Grizabella, the old dying cat, could ascend into the ceiling and go up to the heaven-side lair.

How really crazy was David Merrick at the time? The man who once had five hits running on Broadway simultaneously now concentrated on his extravaganza. I remember him outside of Phil Smith's office, waiting to talk to him.

Mr. Merrick was facing the wall about six inches away, practicing what he was going to say to Smith, Shubert's General Manager. Mr. Smith, who was always well compensated by Shubert, took Merrick into his office for their meeting. A half-hour later, Merrick came out and left.

Then Phil Smith came out to retrieve his phone messages (no phone calls during the meeting with Merrick) and had a look on his face that said on this day, he was devastatingly underpaid.

I would get calls in Jack's office from time to time from a certain woman who called herself Vicki French.

"How was Jack doing? Was he coming back soon?"

I asked the Majestic treasurer Dick Cobb, "Who is she?"

"She's his girlfriend," Dick said.

"At ninety-five?" I asked.

"Why not?" Dick replied.

Jack would occasionally call in to see how things were going. I told him about Vicki French's phone calls.

"Don't tell her where I am, and don't give her my number," he said.

I knew Jack was married, and I completely understood.

***

It was after a matinee, and Mr. Merrick had come to see the condition of his show. I was standing in the grand lobby of the Majestic along with the show's General Manager, Leo Cohen.

Mr. Merrick came over to us with his fedora on and, through his prominent mustache, he complained about a fifty-year-old chorus dancer who was not doing the steps right, and had to be fired. Leo said the stage managers had rehearsed him and said he was fine.

At this point Jerry Orbach, the show's star, tall with rounded shoulders, wandered into the lobby. He came over and heard the end of the conversation. Again, the all-powerful Mr. Merrick, now steamed, insisted this chorus dancer couldn't do it anymore and had to be let go.

He was David Merrick, wasn't he?

"Now who wants to be fired with him?" he asked.

Where was a fifty-year-old tap dancer going to find work like this on Broadway? Merrick walked off and when he was out of earshot Jerry Orbach said: "Merrick will never get a heart attack. He's a carrier."

Leo Cohen told me this story a few years later: he and Merrick were in London watching the new sensation, *Miss Saigon*. Now, you must know the thing about *42nd Street*, Merrick's show, was that it was spectacular, a large cast of fifty, large sets of giant coins, railroad cars, New York streets. Well, when the helicopter in Miss Saigon came down in the second act, Merrick leaned over and poked Leo in the ribs and said: "Finally, something!"

***

I was told Jack Yorke had decided to retire, and that the theatre was going to be given to Spofford Beetle, a senior Shubert manager. I was going back to the Lyceum, since it now had a new booking.

Our play *As Is* struggled through the fall and into the winter. The producer John Glines, who had first put on *Torch Song Trilogy* with Harvey Fierstein to Tony-winning success, could not find a way to sell this wonderful show about the relationship of two gay men, one of whom comes down with AIDS, which was a taboo subject at the time.

I spoke to several people who were leery of seeing the show. One said they feared "those people" might be in the audience, and "who really knows how it is spread?"

It was all silly, ridiculous, and highly offensive. But it was how some people truly felt.

AIDS was such a devastating disease in those days. People who contracted it were often gone so quickly. It was a time of great bravery on the part of the gay community, with a government preoccupied with other things.

Glines came up with the idea for a promotion. In the middle of December, right before Christmas, he planned to give anyone who showed up at the Theatre free tickets to a matinee performance. Sadly, less than two hundred people showed up.

Doctor Ruth, the famed television sex therapist, was not afraid. She had survived the holocaust after all. I took her backstage, and I watched her holding court with lead actors, Jonathan Hadary and Jonathan Hogan, surrounded by crew, dressers, and anyone who worked the show. She told them both they could be on her sex-centered television show, and one could play "impotence" and the other "premature ejaculation."

To which Hadary replied in front of all gathered: "It must be on my face!"

Sadly, the show closed after 285 performances, even though it received a Tony nomination for Best Play in 1985. It was a brave, brave play about courage in a time of fear.

I'd witnessed firsthand this disease devastate the acting community in New York. I had a friend who lived down the hall from me, Court Miller. He was married to a female attorney. Now Court was beautiful, tall, fit, though slightly balding. They seemed quite happy when I would run into them on the elevator of the building. Court had gotten a nice part in *Touch Song Trilogy* on Broadway.

One day in the gym at Manhattan Plaza, he saw me and began talking about a wonderful play he had just seen called *Cloud Nine* by Cheryl Churchill. It was about men and women changing sexual roles.

"This play is really where it's at," he said. Then, he added: "I'm sorry to tell you my wife and I are splitting up. We're doing that because I've decided I'm really gay."

I was flabbergasted. Court projected a very calm and cool masculinity.

Was he really gay?

In the theatre we respect someone's choice. He was a fine actor, and for all I knew, a good man. He really was not seeking my approval, simply telling me what was going on, in case I should wonder why I was not seeing him on the sixth floor of our building anymore.

Eight months later, he was dead from AIDS.

That's how quickly AIDS could strike and kill. He was the first person I knew to die from it, and I distinctly remember his memorial service on the stage of what was the Little Theatre, on 44th Street where *Torch Song* played. Harvey Fierstein gave the eulogy, his gravelly voice filled with tears.

Court Miller, gone too soon, as so many I was to know over the years. People who died for no more than the desire to love.

Lord of the Flops

ONE MORNING IN 1979, I entered "the Blue Room"—the office of legendary producer Alexander H. Cohen—and found him sitting there already going through the pile of mail. His body language was saying, "This is a very sexy, exciting thing."

He was raising the money to do a musical version of the John van Druten play *I Remember Mama*. A very old Richard Rodgers was writing the music. Martin Charnin, who had just directed the smash *Annie,* was staging it, and Thomas Meehan, who had done the book for *Annie*, was writing the book for our show.

The budget was a million dollars.

I had moved up the ladder from the American Place theatre where, after being in a small part or two in their plays, I became the theatre manager. Then I moved on to the Cohen office. Broadway.

Mr. Cohen had a slight touch of Zero Mostel's money-mad character in *The Producers*, which I couldn't criticize because the budget was, after all, a million dollars. He would eventually get over 350 people to invest in *Mama*, so opening the mail and finding a check for fifteen hundred dollars was like prospecting for gold after the thousands and thousands of phone calls he would make to anyone he had ever met in his life.

Today, many modern Broadway producers just write a check for their participation. Alex raised the money for the shows he produced by calling thousands of people, with class and style. He got shows on while never having a smash like *Hello Dolly*, as David Merrick had. A mega-hit like that can fund a decade of producing.

At one point sometime later, I mentioned to him that I noticed he made 450 calls a day, which amazed me. His reply was this: "I return every call I get. I would return Hitler's phone call just to say fuck you!"

He was tough, yes, but it was in a thousand-dollar suit, with manicured hands, and expensive cologne. Class was what he sold, along with the allure and glamor of Broadway.

His track record as a producer had been spotty at best; he had a *New York Magazine* article written about him with the screaming headline: *"Lord of the Flops."*

The last thing I will say in his defense is this: despite his gruff and tough exterior, there was a kindness to him. He wasn't born to a fortune. He had to hustle for every penny, and he was good at it. He started as a watch salesman before he moved on to Broadway, first as a manager, then as a producer.

Every morning, I would bring in an egg on a roll for breakfast. Mr. Cohen would sit there watching me eat it. He was on a bland diet on doctor's orders for his ulcerative stomach.

After a minute or two, he would throw a five-dollar bill at me and say, "Go across the street and get me one of those. To hell with the diet."

He once replied to a doctor who had told him to lose a little weight, "You know how many fine restaurants I have dined in, and how much money I've spent? Good food, good life."

Years later, after Alex had passed, Mike Nichols said to me, "Alex was just a conman."

Alex once called Nichols up, asking him if he would attend the Tonys that coming Sunday night.

Nichols was up for the Best Director award for a play.

Mike replied that his latest film project (perhaps *The Graduate*?) was behind.

"I can't leave the set here in California," he explained.

Then Alex said to him, "Oh, Mike, I think you'll be so disappointed if you don't attend the awards in New York."

Nichols told me, "That's how I knew I was going to win. The hell with a secret ballot! Alex was putting on a television show. That happened about four times."

Perhaps *conman* was stretching things a bit, but I could see where Nichols was coming from. Despite all the flops, Alex always had the money for his apartment on Sloan Street in London, his place on West 54th Street across from the garden of the Museum of Modern Art, his chateau in the south of France, and his chauffeur and limo parked in Shubert Alley. Most of that was from being the yearly producer of the Tony Awards on CBS.

He was the *"Lord of the Flops,"* indeed, but as I once remembered him saying, "I once had a blurb put in the papers that I was going to build the largest sign in history on Times Square, and Al Weise from Van Wagner advertising, whose business it is to construct those signs, called me up. I told him, 'I have no intention to do any such thing. I just wanted to get my name in the paper!' The only thing I cared about was that they spelled my name correctly. Because, if they put your name in the newspaper, they know who you are."

Everything about their success was in the fine print. Alex called me to bring the *Mama* contract to the Shubert executive offices. The attendant, Johnny Dollar, took me down one floor on "his" elevator to a place I had never been. These were the offices of Jacobs and Schoenfeld: the Shubert bosses. They were ornate, with mahogany inlaid wood on the walls and ceiling.

Tony Awards and citations from the City crowded the shelves. I was ushered into Bernie Jacobs' office by his secretary. He and Alex sat across from each other at an oak desk of carved woods. They both read a section of the contract. Alex then said, "You see I'm right."

"But I'm right, too," said Jacobs. "Read the clause again."

Bernie was often accused of being dour, even downright sullen. But when he spoke, an impish grin would often come across his face, betraying a subtle and ever-present sense of humor.

I was thanked by Alex and sent back upstairs.

The Blue Room Boys brigade was the best graduate school for show business going.

First, we got to see Alexander Cohen in all his operating glory. If Alex made a phone call, he wanted a document about the conversation within an hour on the individual's desk. I once had to run a contract up to the Algonquin Hotel to Peter Ustinov, the great actor and raconteur.

I always had a fondness for what he said when he won the Academy Award for *Spartacus*.

"Forgive me if I am underwhelmed. I was at Dunkirk."

Then to me, "Well, everything is perspective. Awards are nice, but living through battle and surviving..."

My fellow Boys were: Gerry and Chris Cohen, Alex's sons; Patrick Maloney, a wonderful crazy Irishman from New Jersey, who became a lifelong friend; and Michael Katz, also a good friend, who became Regis Philbin and Cathy Lee's television producer before becoming an A&E television vice president.

Pat and Gerry became television directors, Gerry directing most of the episodes of the hit sit-com *Married with Children*. Chris soon became my best friend and even ended up my best man when I married in 1982.

Riding up in the elevator, returning from my many deliveries, I often rode with the bosses Schoenfeld and Jacobs. Their knowing me would shortly prove advantageous.

That winter passed by quickly, and then it was time to go to Philadelphia where *I Remember Mama* was to tryout at the Shubert Theatre on Broad Street. We had the great European actress in Liv Ullmann—the muse of Ingmar Bergman himself—playing

"Mama," joined by George Hearn and George S. Irving in the other leading roles. Yes, Liv Ullman was going to sing!

The music was to be composed by the living legend Richard Rogers, who was on his proverbial last legs as he fought throat cancer, which rendered his voice gravelly. Riding with Alex in his limo up to Rudolf Nureyev's townhome to sign a contract for one of Alex's TV shows, out of the blue he turned to me and said: "You know I don't like doing this commercial stuff." Meaning *Mama,* a show which was to prove a lot less than commercial.

"Oh, yes, Mr Cohen, you produced Richard Burton in *Hamlet,* and all of Harold Pinter's plays in *America,*" I replied like a good "yes" man. There was a long pause, as long as one of Pinter's famous pauses in his plays.

"Yeah, but Pinter is full of shit!" Alex retorted.

Alex's stage manager on *Mama* was Jerry Adler, a big, larger-than-life man. Johnny Dollar's special nickname for him was "The Shuffler." Years later, Jerry would find great success in movies and television after sixty.

His wife at the time asked him to pester friends who were producing a movie about Weegee, the crime scene photographer, if there was a part in the movie for her.

The female producer of the film said, "No, Jerry. But I think there might be a part for you, if you are interested."

He read for the part and got it. Now a new world opened up for Jerry he could have never imagined. He was cast in the role of Joe Pesci's editor in the movie *The Private Eye.*

After that, he was cast as the killer in Woody Allen's *Manhattan Murder Mystery*, and later as Hesch in *The Sopranos*, for its six-year run, all after the age of sixty.

But now, as our stage manager, he gave me ten things to do that had to be done by the end of the day.

"I'll try," I replied politely.

"Don't try. Do. You'll find a day is a very long time."

Then Jerry said, "Wait until the Tony Awards. We work so hard dust comes out of mouths."

Next, the entire office was off to Philadelphia for an out-of-town tryout of *Mama*. It was early March, and the winter broke into a beautiful string of early spring days in 1979. Though the weather was beautiful, the show was not. Problems persisted from the very beginning, despite Richard Rogers' soaring music.

Singing was not Liv's gift, even though Alex's crush on her remained constant. It was a platonic crush, as he had on so many actresses over the years.

With the show in trouble, it did not help that Martin Charnin gave Liv Ullmann instruction over a microphone from the twentieth row of the orchestra. This is the woman who was used to taking directions for a master of cinema, let's not forget.

Ingmar Bergman, the great Swedish director, and her lover, would sleep with her to get her to do a scene slightly differently.

"No, no, Liv. Don't go over there, stay stage center," Marty would go over the mike. "Come on, Liv. Remember your blocking."

They had begun shouting at each other in rehearsal, and something had to be done.

"Marty has to go," Alex whispered. So, he fired him.

By then, Charlie Willard, the company manager, had taken me as his non-contractual assistant manager. That meant that the dirty work was, suddenly, mine.

He gave me Marty's last check: "Take it over to him."

I gingerly knocked on Marty's hotel room door... and there he was, the saddest man in the world. You see, despite the enormous success of *Annie*, his previous several productions—*Hot Spot, Mata Hari, Nash at Nine*—had all failed. He was back to that, despite the fact we Blue Room Boys figured he was making over $30,000 a week in royalties from the seven touring productions of *Annie* in 1979 going around the world.

As I quickly turned to go, he said, "Wait for me. I have to go to the office to get some things."

It was my first lesson in the fact that the business is about how your last show did.

Failure is a blackbird that can land on your shoulder at any time. I walked with a heartbroken man back to our office in the enormous Shubert Theatre. In comparison, I was making $200 a week and was so happy to be a part of it all.

All the Blue Room Boys had moved into a beautiful townhome on Locust Street. Nightly parties took place when we weren't hanging out at the bar of the Drake Hotel.

Liv Ullman's fourteen-year-old daughter loved to hang out with us. We were the cool guys, and she wanted to be with us and the many teen actors who were in the show's cast.

We were totally respectful, treating her as a little sister. But, let me tell you, it was odd to have an international movie star like Ms. Ullman knock on your door to retrieve her daughter at ten at night. The look she gave us was Oscar-worthy.

In the midst of all this, one afternoon I went into the bathroom only to be followed by Richard Rodgers. He shuffled up to a urinal two away from me.

What to say to a living legend like the composer of *Oklahoma, The King and I,* and *South Pacific?*

"Have you finished the new song yet?"

"Not yet," in his horse voice. "Show sure needs it, doesn't it?"

He had produced thirty Broadway Shows and knew this one was in trouble. Alex hired Cy Furer, of *Guys and Dolls* fame, to direct after Martin Charnin's dismissal.

The first thing Cy wanted to do was watch the original film of *Mama* with Irene Dunn.

I volunteered for the job.

I had been in the audiovisual department in junior high and I got a projector up to Cy's hotel room. I then threaded it, focused it on a wall, and pulled down the shades. Cy and his wife watched intently.

He had seen the show the night before and wanted to know where we went so wrong. What was missing was the incredible charm of those late forties movies: Irene Dunn's simple, beautiful performance, and the style of movies in those days.

***

It had become a very terrifying time in Philadelphia. The hydrogen bubble was in the reactor at Three Mile Island. If it exploded, and the wind was blowing our way... well, how a Broadway show's tryout was going would have been of little concern. There was sullen fear on faces as you walked the streets of Philadelphia.

It was right at this time the boss of the Shubert was coming to town to see the production. He had given Alex the Majestic Theatre for *Mama* and wanted to see what was up.

Gerry Schoenfeld was a short, stocky man who exuded the power of his position. Alex dispatched me along with Carry, his limo driver, to meet Mr. Schoenfeld at the train station and to take him to the theatre.

It was still called the Shubert Theatre, but no longer owned by the organization. They had to divest many of their properties after an anti-trust ruling against the Shubert brothers came down in the mid-1950s. They were ruled then to be a controlling monopoly of American theatre, owning most of the legitimate houses across the country.

We passed by a hospital and Gerry pointed up at a room on a high floor of the place. It was the only time in the over thirty years of working for him that I ever saw a look of total terror come over his face.

"That's where Zero died," he said, meaning Zero Mostel, the legendary actor and crazy man who he had produced in *The Merchant*.

To lighten the mood, I told him a joke—one that Jerry Adler had told us the day before in our office above the theatre on Broad Street. It worked its magic. He roared at the joke and that broke the ice between us.

I was next given the task of taking George Hearn's latest check to the Drake Hotel to pay for the $853 he owed on his bar tab. The Drake was the company's hotel and at night George could be found buying drinks, leaning against the bar, and singing "Danny Boy" with his golden voice at two in the morning. We—the show—had to pay this bill so George could leave Philadelphia without debt collectors in close pursuit as we returned to New York.

Within a day or so, I got a call from Peter Entin, from Shubert Theatre Operations.

"An apprenticeship for a theatre manager had opened up. Would you be interested in taking it?" he asked.

I told Alex Cohen. Ever eager to shed another from the payroll of his failing show, he shouted—and I mean shouted—"Go!"

The Blue Room Boys said telling Gerry Schoenfeld that joke was what got me the job. They threw me a wild party for my leaving the show. Chris Cohen, a mad raging bull of a man, drank twenty-eight shots of Bushmills Irish whiskey, one for each year of my age, to toast my departure. Crazy, yes, but true.

Many of Maloney's friends, as he was a Jersey Shore boy, had come down to drink and party, too. One such reveler ran out into the street with perfect timing as he proceeded to throw up on a passing Volkswagen.

By the end of our stay at Locust Street, the four inhabitants of the house had destroyed the curtains of a beautiful canopied bed, broken dishes, glasses, and lamps. For six weeks, it was our own private National Lampoon Animal House.

The bill to repair the house and things we had destroyed at the end of the run in Philadelphia was $7,000. Alex paid it, called it a "production expense," and moved on.

The next day I left Philadelphia, with the hydrogen bubble still in the reactor. Had it exploded, it still might not have been as big a bomb as *I Remember Mama.*

In fact, Thomas Meehan, the show's book writer, who later went on to pen the books for such smash musicals as *Hairspray and The Producers,* was fond of saying, because of all the directors, actors, and costumers that Alex fired on the show: "More people came back alive from Vietnam than Philadelphia."

Because I know you're wondering... this is the joke I told Gerry Schoenfeld.

Jerry Adler was the assistant stage manager on the original production of *My Fair Lady* with Rex Harrison and Julie Andrews.

Phil Adler, his father, was the General Manager of the show. Is there nepotism in show business? Yes, every day, in every way.

The legendary Moss Hart was the director of the show. Moss had been in the hospital for a stay and now he was out. He had promised friends who were doing a show in a Maryland summer theatre that he would come and see it if he could. He called Jerry up and asked him to ride along in his limo to see the show.

Jerry could not refuse, even though it was his day off. So, a young Jerry and an old Moss Hart rode down to Maryland to this theatre out in the sticks. They were late, but since the people involved in the show knew Moss Hart was coming, they held the curtain.

With Mr. Hart finally in his seat, they began the show. The play was about a leprechaun, and in the second scene, he swung onstage holding a rope. However, the rope tangled around his hand and he couldn't get free.

He swung back and forth madly, trying to get loose of the thing. On the second swing, he struck a flat on the set. As he swung back, he struck another, and that flat started to collapse onto the stage.

They hurriedly brought the curtain down. Moss Hart immediately got up and rushed out of the theatre with Jerry close behind. In the limo, he told his driver to return to New York.

Mr. Hart turned to Jerry and then said: "It was short, but I liked it."

Bob Fosse and Mozart

THE NEXT MONDAY MORNING, after putting on my one good suit, I made my way to 234 West 44th Street, Shubert's executive offices. I was told to wait outside Peter Entin's office.

Through the windows, across the street, the giant Shubert Theatre loomed. Peter was the Theatre Operations manager, and I was to be his assistant as an apprentice manager. Peter held the contract on the Broadhurst Theatre across the street where Bob Fosse's hit musical *Dancin'* was playing.

A highly intelligent man, who was both a Cornell and Yale graduate, Peter measured his words carefully, often leaving you waiting ten seconds.

"How's your math?" he asked.

"I can use a calculator."

"How's your writing?"

"I check everything twice before I send it in."

That was a lie.

"Gerry likes you."

"I'm glad. He's the boss, isn't he?"

"Yeah," Peter said, as a look of exhaustion crossed his face. Then he said something very profound; something I was to find to be so very true over the many coming years, which was: "The hardest thing about the job is the monotony. Six days a week, week after week, we do the same thing."

I couldn't believe he was talking about the bright lights of Broadway.

"On a long run it's a little like going to a factory," he continued, "when the only time you notice anything is when it's different, when it's wrong. Onstage, or in the theatre, I mean."

I nodded, trying to understand and listen.

"One last thing. Don't shit where you eat." Translation: leave the dancers in the show alone, no matter how beautiful.

He rose from behind his heavy oak desk. I followed him across the street to the Broadhurst's stage door.

"And don't tell them how old you are," Peter concluded, meaning the Local One crew, the grizzly old stagehands.

I looked younger than my twenty-eight years. I would find out later that Peter was from my neck of the woods: Queens, namely Hollis, or Queens Village. We had both attended junior high school 109; at different times, of course, because he was a few years older.

Inside the theatre, Peter beckoned over a short man I was taking over from and introduced him as Bob La Prince. It was immediately obvious that Bob was flamboyantly gay. Bob took me through the ins and outs of the job: the payroll, box office, the cleaners and porters, the ushers, musicians, and, of course, the stagehands.

He wished me luck on dealing with the last part of the gig: irate patrons. After a week or so, I was on my own.

The show *Dancin'* was amazing. It included a series of incredibly difficult Bob Fosse choreographed dance numbers, performed by Fosse dancers, who were the best show dancers in the world. Ann Reinking, Vicki Frederick, Sandal Bergman, Gail Benedict, Wayne Cilento, John Mineo.

They moved from isolation to isolation, then to leg kicks, spins, and contortions. It all ended with a ten-minute solo to the music of "Sing, Sing, Sing" delivered by Ms. Reinking to cheers of amazement. It was unreal how Annie could go from one move to the other. Her sheer speed at doing so was inspiring and beautiful to behold.

The dancers often hurt themselves with sprains and pulled muscles, no matter how they warmed up.

As the company manager G. Warren McClane said, "There were so many injuries it was like running a football team."

We all called him Warren, which he preferred because the "G" stood for George and, coincidentally, this wonderful gay gentleman of the theatre bore an uncanny resemblance to George Washington. We both had worked with Alexander Cohen, which was a great ice-breaker.

We remained friends throughout our lives.

He turned to me that day and said, "I was once staying the weekend at his farm in Connecticut. He was commenting to his son, Gerry, who was perhaps seven or eight years old. He said about the Times theatre critic: 'Walter Kerr is a bore! Do you know what a bore is, Gerry?' And his son replied: 'A wild pig!' Alex turned to me and said, 'Top that!'"

About six months into my being on the show, when I was counting the afternoon's box office, I was called to the back of the orchestra. I was told that a stubborn drunk was insisting on a Scotch even though the bar was long closed, with the show in full swing.

I left the box office and went to the bar to see a short man wearing a hat crooked to the side, with a lit cigarette dangling in his mouth... in a no-smoking theatre! He was also dropping twenty-dollar bills on the floor from a very large roll in his hand.

I said to the bartender, "This is Mr. Fosse. Give him what he wants."

"A double," Fosse said. He took his dangling cigarette and his drink and went over and leaned on the back wall of the orchestra from where he watched his show.

After that, when I passed him on the street, I would always get a big, "Hi, Dan."

I would've been flattered, except of course he wasn't going to forget the name of the guy who could open the bar for him in the middle of the show.

***

Gwen Verdon, the legendary Broadway star of such shows as *Damn Yankees* and *Chicago*, was the dance captain. She was there nightly, along with Nicole, the daughter she shared with Fosse.

Perhaps that's why Bob needed a double scotch to watch his own show on a Wednesday afternoon. He was surrounded by his many romantic entanglements! He had been with Ann Reinking, his star in the show, along with other women of his ensemble he was famous for coming on to.

We call it "A Straight Dancer"—deadly in the business of Broadway where so many male dances are gay.

I, at first hand, witnessed how Fosse could be cruel to his women. I walked into the stage door during one matinee and spotted Ann Reinking at the pay phone, crying uncontrollably and screaming into the receiver: "Don't you ever call me like this again!"

I went down to the stage manager's room office and reported it. Sitting there unperturbed, Perry Klein said: "Oh, that's just Fosse telling her she's too fat to do his show."

And this was a few minutes before she had to go on!

Talk about knocking the confidence out of someone. Maybe Annie had gained five pounds, but she was still the best dancer you'd ever seen. She was the very heart and soul of the show. Her last performance in that show was both terrible and wonderful in equal measure.

It occurred around Christmas, just as her contract was ending with the New Year. Down in the basement, below the stage, we had a curtained off an area where the dancers could warm up. There they were hidden from the crew members and the gaze of the horny musicians.

Annie had just finished her warm-up routine and was on her way out of the tented area when Michael Kubala, a big, strong, six-foot-three male dancer, strode in like the giant he was.

To avoid colliding with him, Ann had gone down out of the way. Her knee struck the bottom of the metal post in the basement that held up the curtained space. The sharp corner put a large gash in her knee.

The dancers stood around her, horrified at what had happened. But Ann was a big believer in the old adage, "The show must go on."

So, instead of pulling out of the performance, she had her dresser wrap up her knee hurriedly in an Ace bandage. She went on, probably knowing that this may well be her last performance in the show Fosse created for her.

At the intermission, her dresser pulled down her leotard and ripped the bandage off her knee, which was now soaked in blood. She wrapped Ann's knee up again with a new bandage before she went back out to finish the show, including her solo in the finale, "Sing, Sing, Sing."

Afterward, Ann went to the hospital and had her wound stitched up. She never performed in *Dancin'* again.

She choreographed and created the new edition of *Chicago* a decade later. Bearing no grudge, she even hired Michael Kubala to perform in it, which speaks volumes about her.

It hit me hard when I heard of her sudden passing while I was in the middle of writing this memoir. My abiding memory of her is as a young and strong dancer in her prime. It was like losing a great athlete in high school when you were eternally young—with death even in seventy years seeming impossible.

In the fall of 1980, *Dancin'* was moved to the Ambassador Theatre to make way for a hit from England entitled *Amadeus* by Peter Shaffer. Shaffer had written the recent smash *Equus*, along with a string of other hits.

Amadeus, a drama about the rivalry between Mozart and the minor composer Antonio Salieri, starred Ian McKellen as Salieri, Tim Curry as Mozart, and Jane Seymour as Constanze, Mozart's wife. The story of the genius Mozart's troubled life and early death was an immediate smash with lines of ticket buyers down the block.

Peter Shaffer, a true commercial playwright, would stand outside the lobby of the Broadhurst Theatre and literally count the people queuing to get in. His brother Anthony Shaffer had another enormous hit in *Sleuth,* later made into a movie starring Michael Caine and Laurence Olivier.

The Shaffers were identical twins, and both wore old British schoolboy coats with toggle buttons and hoods, even though they were both grey-haired and in their fifties. They also both wore heavy-rimmed glasses, which made them almost indistinguishable unless you were acquainted with either. They were the toast of London and Broadway in those days of the late seventies and early eighties.

One matinee in the early days of the run, a lady had sneaked in under a heavy coat her very young baby. Suddenly, in the middle of the first act, the baby awoke and started crying. The young male usher, a substitute, poorly trained, heard the baby but let the child cry for ten minutes before I was called.

After refunding her ticket, I made the young mother leave. At show's end, I was called back to Ian's dressing room and read the riot act.

I profusely apologized and said it would never happen again, feeling totally humiliated.

Here we come to the first rule of theatre management: never take the word of a young mother that her baby will not cry. Infants do not know the decorum of theatre, or care. You will hear from fifty patrons about the crying baby, and in the worst case, from your star. Should all these things happen more than once, seek other employment.

The legendary husband and wife team of Paul Newman and Woodward came by to see the show and requested to go backstage to meet Ian after the performance.

On entering Ian's dressing room, Joanne, ever the gracious southern lady, said: "This was so marvelous."

Paul, who was half in his cups from the beer he so enjoyed, said, "Yeah, you really kicked us in the ass with this one!"

Ian, the consummate English gentleman, nodded his head and replied, "Thank you. I loved you in *The Sting.*"

At that, I took an early exit, not wanting to see where the conversation went from there. It was toward the end of Ian's run in the show that he agreed to do his one-man show *Acting Shakespeare* in a benefit for the Second Stage Theatre Company. I was given the task of general managing the presentation. Ian was brilliant, as he went through numerous characters and plays, and the presentation was a sold-out success.

The very special guests at the benefit were Princess Grace, the former Grace Kelly, and Prince Rainier of Monaco. Sixty paparazzi had gathered outside the Broadhurst Theatre waiting to get their shot of the royal couple.

The Prince and Princess Grace got out of their limousine about eighty feet from the marquee of the Broadhurst. They started walking toward the lobby and front entrance doors, perhaps to avoid all the cameras.

Princess Grace made it to the entrance and entered, but then the paparazzi recognized what was happening and crashed into the lobby with cameras flashing. They trapped Prince Rainier just outside the theatre entrance. Then, like King Kong or Samson, he shrugged his large shoulders and parted the sea of madness in order to enter.

Amadeus deservedly won the Tony for best play that June. Ian McKellen took home the Best Actor Tony as well.

Jacqueline Bisset came to see the show, and I took her backstage to Jane Seymour's dressing room afterward. As I left them alone, I walked back out to the hallway to find Tim Curry, who looked intrigued.

"There went Jacqueline Bisset, the good time had by all," he remarked to my startled face. Tim was a card, wonderful as the child genius Mozart. That playful impishness was part of his very soul.

I met a couple of young ladies a short time later who were massive Tim Curry fans, thanks to his madcap performance as the transvestite Frank-n-Furter in *The Rocky Horror Show*. I bought them a couple of tickets to the show and asked Tim if he would like to go out for a drink with us.

"A quick one, yes," he replied.

It was quicker than I could've imagined. We went to Joe Allen's and sat in the backyard garden. After our drinks were knocked back and the bill paid, I went to the bathroom before we left, ready to make my move on the one I fancied. When I came back out, everyone was gone.

As I walked to my home alone, I thought to myself, "Well, there's just something that drives women crazy about a man who can wear fishnet stockings that well."

***

At the end of the summer, we were all invited to dinner at the Dish of Salt restaurant as Ian, Tim Curry, and Jane Seymour ended their run in the show. Jane jokingly asked me, "Can you get me a job selling show programs at the back of the theatre?"

"It would be a much harder job than playing Constanze," I quipped.

She would, of course, go on to become the television mini-series queen in Hollywood and London.

The trio were replaced by legendary English actors John Wood and Peter Firth, who was the original boy in *Equus*, alongside Amy

Irving, who had started to make a name for herself in movies. They and the show were well-reviewed again. Peter Shaffer, ever the commercial playwright, insisted that a quote board of those reviews would be good for sales.

So, such a quote board was put in the lobby. But about a week later, it disappeared. Then it worked like this: Peter Shaffer called Gerry Schoenfeld, Gerry called Peter Entin, and he asked me, "What happened to the quote sign?"

I said something like, "Isn't it there?"

"No, Peter Shaffer, who was only now standing outside the theatre lobby, said it was gone."

I was the detective put in charge of this mystery. I asked the doorman and the stagehands if had they seen it, or seen someone take it.

After a couple of days, the stage doorman let me in on the theatre-wide secret: Amy Irving had taken the sign and hid it up high on the stairway immediately to the right of the doorman's booth. It was just a staircase to the roof, with no dressing rooms up there.

She had taken the sign up there because of a quote on the board that screamed: "Amy Irving's Constanze is kittenish."

Taking umbrage, she had carried this rather large sign all by herself to the top of the column where only engineers were allowed to go and leaned it against the wall up there.

I placed it back in the lobby, this time chained to a door. Not long after, I was called on a Sunday matinee to Peter Firth's dressing room backstage. Amy sat with her back to me as Peter rambled on about how hot the theatre was, and how they were in these period costumes under the blazing stage lights.

In the mirror, I saw Amy's eyes burning into me as Firth angrily went on and on. I promised to make it as cool as I could.

Amy did not ask me for a job at the end of her run in the show selling programs because soon she hit the jackpot when she married Steven Spielberg. Six years later, they divorced, and it was reported Amy received a settlement in the vicinity of one hundred million dollars.

A burly stagehand with many children, who had worked on the show with both of us, said to me: "Hell, I would have married him for that."

***

January 9, 1982, was the day I married a beautiful redhead from Miami named Lyle. We held our reception on the fourth floor of Sardi's so all of my theatre friends could drop in between shows and have a drink.

At a small table in the rear, Gerry Schoenfeld and Phil Smith, Shubert's chairman and general manager, sat alone.

I was getting the feeling I had made the team at Shubert and that I would be offered a job after my apprenticeship was over. I would later find out that Gerry Schoenfeld had said, "I don't want Dan Landon leaving this company."

Which was obviously very flattering.

"You have turned the corner," Peter Entin said, meaning in his eyes I had straightened up and learned how to fly right.

Now all I had to do was pass the manager's test. And I did so with flying colors, getting a 94, the second-highest grade of my year.

I was called again into Phil Smith's office.

"Well, all I have to offer you is the Lyceum Theatre," he said matter-of-factly. Desperate to continue working on Broadway, I did not hesitate to grab the opportunity.

Soon after, I was in Peter Entin's office and it was arranged for me to take over at the Lyceum. I knew the theatre. Correction: I loved that theatre. I had been assigned to do eighty-six-year-old Archie Thompson's paperwork for $40 a week as an extra job. I would meet Archie at the Lyceum.

He had been the Shubert brothers' stage manager of their self-produced shows in the 1930s and was in the Shubert will, which meant he couldn't be fired without great cause. Archie, a flamboyant character in beautiful silk suits, all of which were easily thirty years old but still pristine, was fond of saying to Mary Levins, the local West Side woman who was in charge of hiring all the ushers: "I like girly men and boyish girls. Send me those."

He had been one of the soldiers who carried John Barrymore offstage at the end of his 1926 production of *Hamlet*. He had seen it all and done it all, except now his paperwork: his payroll, settlement, union pension forms, etc.

He told me stories about the late handsome John Barrymore, the man who looked out a New York bar window one afternoon and said: "So many women, so little time."

Archie had recently passed away several months before my managerial apprenticeship was over.

There was a scene in the second act of *Amadeus* when the Emperor of Austria, played by Nicholas Kepros, complains to Mozart that there are too many notes in his symphony. Mozart replies, "There are as many notes as are required, Majesty."

After an awkward silence, the Emperor states, "Well, there it is!"

"Well, there it is!" said Entin, sending me off as a full-fledged union manager now. It was to be our "catchphrase" for years to come.

My father would come by and knock on the Lyceum box office window and we would go to lunch. Or more often, he would just borrow forty dollars and be on his way.

Growing up on Long Island, I caught the acting bug early in high school. It seemed to be the only way I could earn any respect from my father. I was an average football player at best, but on stage in *My Sister Eileen* and *The Miracle Worker*, he said I was a good actor.

Do you remember the popular HBO TV series *Mad Men*? The slang term was an all-too-clever abbreviation for those advertisers who spent their days working on Madison Avenue and their nights enjoying the nightlife of New York. You wouldn't go too far wrong with picturing my father as one of those men.

He also was one of the foremost writers of industrial musical shows, which were the rah-rah productions that companies would organize in-house for their employees. In 1969, the biggest industrial extravaganza in Manhattan was the *Milliken Textile Show,* and my dad wrote it, with a budget of $3 million.

Now, to put this into perspective, the most expensive Broadway musical of the day was produced to the tune of $1 million. Michael Bennett was the director of the show, soon to be the director of *A Chorus Line* for fame and fortune. The composer of the Milliken show was Marvin Hamlisch, also of *A Chorus Line.* My father may never have received a Tony nomination or award as they did, but he did create the Esso tiger in an industrial show with the famous slogan*: Put a tiger in your tank.*

He liked to joke that he was—wait for it—a "roaring success" in his chosen profession. And, to give him his due, he was. However, he was an absent father. Though he was making big money from those shows, the lights in our little Cape Cod home would go off because the bill was unpaid, much to my mother's dismay, the beautiful girl he made his bride when he was in the Army and a journalist for *The Stars and Stripes* newspaper in 1949 in Germany.

But when he was home, his approval and presence were everything to me.

My father was not the first member of the Landon family to work in showbiz. His two brothers, Daniel and Donald, were handsome 12-year-old twin boys with voices like angels when they got to tread the boards on Broadway in a production of *The Man Who Came to Dinner* by Moss Hart and George S. Kaufman.

My father was their understudy.

They might have "only" been two of the choirboys who come onstage in the third act, but they received a combined salary of a phenomenal $100 a week, which was about four times greater than the average wage in the late 1930s.

It pulled my family out of the crushing poverty they had experienced through the Great Depression.

The alcohol had taken his career and health by the time he was coming to the Lyceum box office window and asking for me. There was a feeling that we had come full circle. His son was working on Broadway, and that was a good thing that made him proud.

Bernadette and Bobby

PETER ENTIN SUMMONED ME to his office. He had a look on his face that screamed: *Why me, Lord?*

"I need you to go work at the Royale," he said.

The Mackintosh musical *Song and Dance* was playing over at the beautiful theatre with its Victoria-style architecture. The regular manager, Bill Lieberman, had gotten into near physical confrontations with his treasurer, Billy Friendly, who claimed that it was about Lieberman walking in friends to the production. It was odd for Billy to concern himself with something like that.

As a result, they decided to move Lieberman to the Longacre and put me at the Royale.

The show itself featured Bernadette Peters, who was already a major Broadway star. She had been in the movies *Annie*, *The Jerk*, *Pennies From Heaven*, Mel Brook's *Silent Movie*, and went along for the ride in Clint Eastwood's *Pink Cadillac*.

The first half of the musical was about a girl who comes to New York and all the songs were sung by Peters herself. Act Two was a beautiful dance about a young man, played by Christian d'Amboise, who also comes to the big city. It featured the dancers Greg

Mitchell, Scott Wise, Cynthia Onrubia, Denise Faye, Charlotte d'Amboise, the daughter of the legendary choreographer Jacques d'Amboise, and sister of Christian. They would spend their lives dancing in *Chicago, Cats,* and the numerous tours of *A Chorus Line.*

It was Bernadette who held it all together and gave it meaning. Unexpected Song was a hit from the show, and Peters won a Tony for her brilliant performance.

The company manager, Roger Gindi, told me he was under strict instruction not to call Bernadette before noon. Roger reckoned it might have been Bernadette's revenge for having to get up at four every morning to make breakfast for her father, who delivered bread all around in her teenage days, her mother having died years before.

During the run, Bernadette's birthday came along and she threw a grand party at her place on the West Side. Her home was a little house on top of a building with green astroturf covering the whole roof. As you looked out, the lights of the city glowed all around.

I also had a party at my apartment at Manhattan Plaza and invited everyone.

A brief word about Manhattan Plaza, dubbed "Broadway's Bedroom," which allocated 70% of its 1,674 units for people working in the performing arts. Best of all, rents were calculated on a sliding scale based on 25% of one's gross income. It was great for theater folk like myself, as our incomes were so unpredictable and variable.

The developer who constructed Manhattan Plaza's two towers in 1974 on the city block between 42nd and 43rd Streets and 9th and 10th Avenues designed it as middle-class housing with luxury amenities in the complex: an Olympic-sized pool, a fancy gym, a playground, racquetball and tennis courts, underground garage, and essential retailers on the ground floor. However, not enough people wanted to live in the scary neighborhood of "Hell's Kitchen," but that was perfect for people in the performing arts, providing a housing safety net and a ten-minute walk to Broadway. Many who lived there became household names: Larry David, Jack Warden, Loretta Devine, Alicia Keyes, etc.

Back to my party. I offered Charlotte d'Amboise a beer when she walked in the door. She said right away, "Oh, I'm only eighteen. I can't have a beer."

Ironically, for such a goodie two shoes, she was to go on to marry Terry Mann, the wild man of Broadway, who played the Rum Tum Tugger in *Cats*, and Javert in *Les Misérables*.

When I would fill in at *Cats* for the regular manager, Mindy Levine, Terry, in full makeup and costume, would growl at me and show his claws every time I passed him backstage. I thought he was totally nuts.

That night of my party, two stagehands, one of whom was Mike Van Praugh, a house head at the Royale, went up to the top of the building and somehow got on the roof and began throwing the ice from their drinks off into the night. The pieces landed on the outside dining area of the Curtain Up restaurant forty-five floors below. Building security was called to investigate and found the culprits up there. The officers brought both of them to my apartment door.

"Do you know these guys?" they asked me.

"I've never seen them before in my life," I said, doing my best impression of Jack Lemmon as the naïve CC 'Bud' Baxter in *The Apartment*.

"He knows us!" Mike shouted.

"We work together at the theatre," the other protested.

"What theatre?" I said, slamming the door shut in their faces. They were thrown out as the party went on.

***

Across the street from the Royale, there were several so-called theatre bars. The most popular was Sam's, which was named after the proprietor Sam Puleo. Another was Barrymore's, named after the famous, long-gone John Barrymore. Barrymore's was our haunt. Ushers, managers, treasurers, and actors could order a hamburger and fries, and have a cocktail or two, or three, or four.

It was Billy Friendly's favorite place, while other treasurers favored Wally's on 49th Street, or Frankie and Johnny's, where a drunken Jason Robards was once thrown out by the Secret Service for calling a sitting president eating dinner "Tricky Dick."

Between shows one afternoon, I was walking into the theatre's front doors about ten feet behind Billy Friendly, who had crossed into the outer lobby after drinking the afternoon away in Barrymore's.

At the ticket window, Cynthia Onrubia, one of our dancers in the shortest of shorts, was bent over at the window, talking to someone in the box office. Cynthia was twenty, a beautiful and petite Philippine girl. Her mother would come and pick her up at the stage door after her performance, and walk her home the three blocks to their apartment in Manhattan Plaza. Even though she had been on Broadway since she was fifteen, she was nevertheless innocent in manner and behavior. Billy, as he was walking past her, proceeded to bite her on the exposed part of her behind that her short shorts did not cover. She screamed, of course.

Billy had bitten off more than he could chew. Later that night, we were informed by Roger Gindi that the bite had left marks on Cynthia. Roger officially had to inform Peter Entin about the complaint.

It was the first of a long list of shenanigans I would endure with Billy. Now biting a dancer on her bottom would have gotten most people fired, but not Billy. I always wondered what he had on the bosses that protected him. His father Danny, who had been the manager of the Palace, had been good friends with Phil Smith. His godmother was none other than Judy Garland.

He was handsome and strong, a former college basketball player. He wore his wild-man persona during his entire career, but I always wondered who his "Rabbi" was. That's a term for the person who brought you into the business and helped you on the way. He was an excellent treasurer and could move a line of waiting ticket holders five minutes before curtain quicker than anyone I ever worked with, but this incident was not atypical and had to be dealt with.

So, Billy had to leave the Royale. He was sent to the Barrymore, and I back to the Longacre. Bill Liberman returned to his contractual house at the Royale.

At the time, the Longacre show was *Cuba and his Teddy Bear*, starring Robert De Niro, Ralph Macchio, and Burt Young. Within a year I was to move to the Barrymore, where I was to stay when there was a show in residence, for twenty-eight years, mostly with Billy Friendly as the treasurer.

***

At the Longacre, his name was not Mr. De Niro. Or Robert. Or Godfather. His name was Bobby, pure and simple. I had been told of his dislike, no, downright fear of crowds, of strangers. At the end of every night's performance, a bodyguard went down to the edge of the stage just in case someone wanted to shake his hand during the curtain call.

It was 1987, and he was already one of the most famous actors in the world, having appeared in legendary movies like *The Godfather Part II* and *Taxi Driver*. But, around the Longacre Theatre, he was simply Bobby.

Cuba and the Teddy Bear was about a man who is a drug dealer and now has the dilemma of his only son becoming involved in drugs. Burt Young, of *Rocky* fame, played the boy's uncle. Ralph Macchio, The Karate Kid, played De Niro's son. Now, I had seen this fear of the audience before. Al Pacino, at intermission of the performance he was attending, would go behind box curtains to go unnoticed by the audience. It is one thing to say, "Well, who would hurt them?" They were world-famous actors, and beloved.

But then I always thought who would hurt someone like John Lennon, and look what happened.

Celebrities came by in droves the last month of the run, as you can imagine. Mike Tyson, soon to be the heavyweight champion, got lost and wandered all around backstage.

"I was about to go home," Tyson said when I found him. Mike would play the Longacre two decades later with a one-man show, remembering all his lines after a long boxing career.

The engagement proceeded without event until one night, just before the end of the show, the old abandoned tenement next to the firehouse on 48th Street caught on fire.

It was nighttime, and the show was on. The smoke from the fire was drifting eastward over the top of the theatre. Even though I had shut the blowers off and closed the vents, heavy smoke was still getting into the theatre, hanging over the area just below the balcony like a cloud.

It was a small house, thank God, with no one up in the balcony. Had there been, every patron up there would have come to me coughing with watery eyes. I had been standing with an FDNY lieutenant, determining whether we should stop the show.

There were no more than ten minutes left in the play. The fireman and I looked at each other, both of us wondering what to do. Then the lieutenant said, "I'm not stopping De Niro with that much left," and I agreed with him. As soon as the show was over, my porter and I opened the side doors of the theatre and ushered the house out into the street.

The last day of the run, Bobby came to the back of the house and personally thanked me and every usher. He had made it to the end of the run. He had done it. He had beaten back his fear of strangers and crowds.

An actor like De Niro is someone I have often admired. His incredible talent, yes. But his reserved nature did not demand that you treat him any differently from any actor in any show you had ever worked on. He was, after all, simply Bobby, and wanted to be treated that way.

It was a Joe Papp production, and afterward, we were all invited to a party in the lobby of the Public Theater on Lafayette Street. There, the understudies performed a parody of the show.

Bobby sat in the front row with one of his children sitting on his lap. He roared with laughter, as we all did. Over the years I would see him as he came by the Barrymore to see the play that was on, mostly with his good friend Harvey Keitel and their wives.

I would remind him I was the theatre manager during the run of *Cuba and the Teddy Bear* and he always treated me like a long-lost friend.

The last time I saw him, when he came by the Barrymore, I got my camera and asked him for a picture. His son took the picture of us. I then asked if he would ever do another Broadway show.

He said, "Those days are over." Then, after a moment, "But never say never."

My Drinking Buddy

OFTEN BOTH THE BARRYMORE and the Longacre were dark. On those occasions, I was assigned anywhere from a week to a month on shows on 45th Street, such as *Lend Me a* , which was a brilliantly funny farce that takes place in the Cleveland Opera. The late Patrick Quinn played Max, who winds up playing the opera star who becomes too sick to perform. It's one of the funniest plays ever to play Broadway, so we were all discouraged because the Times critic Frank Rich didn't like it and gave it a middling review.

For decades we had made a living working on boulevard comedies like the plays of Neil Simon, and other hits like *There's a Girl in My Soup, Cactus Flower,* and *Don't Drink the Water.* If Rich wasn't going to give them favorable reviews, their future was bleak. In those days the Times was still the so-called paper of record and could make or break a show.

I also worked on Tom Stoppard's *The Real Thing* with Jeremy Irons and Glen Close, which was an enormous hit, to the point that even the great playwright himself was stunned by its success. There were fill-in weeks on the big musicals as well: *Cats, Evita* where Patti LuPone reigned supreme, and *A Chorus Line*—the show that saved Broadway, according to Gerry Schoenfeld.

There were ten or eleven Shubert managers for the sixteen theatres in those days. It just "shows" how many occasions theatres were unbooked for long periods.

Joe Turner's Come and Gone, by August Wilson, next played the Barrymore. It featured Delroy Lindo and a young Angela Bassett, who went on to play Tina Turner in the movie *What's Love Got to do with It?*

When the director Lloyd Richards of *Joe Turner* entered the theatre for the first time, he looked onstage and saw the floor being mopped by the house prop man, John Higgins. Richards told me, "Twenty-five years ago, when I left the theatre when *Raisin in the Sun* was over, the last thing I saw was the same man mopping the stage!"

Welcome to Broadway where house jobs—props, carpentry, electric—are not readily surrendered.

The play, set in the 1900s, was inhabited by the rhythms and sounds of the years just past, the years of Jim Crow. August's dream was to write a play for every decade of the twentieth century. It was before its time with the brilliant broken words moving to the vibrations of African drums surrounded by remembered oppression and the horrors of slavery. Despite positive critical response, the public did not understand it, or take to it.

August discovered the cool place after the theatre in those days was the West Bank Cafe on 42nd Street between 9th and 10th Avenue. There you could see Sean Penn and Madonna at night holding court at a table across the room. I remember once sitting down at the bar with Julianna Margulies on one side and Neve Campbell on the other. August and I ran into each other there one night. I lived upstairs at Manhattan Plaza and would stop down there on occasion for a quick drink on my way home.

After he found that out, I would get a question from him from time to time: "Are you going over to the club tonight?" We'd meet after the show and go over together to have a few. The Irish Mob was in their heyday and a black man walking on 9th Avenue late at night might feel a little uneasy—that was the way I figured the friendship.

I was lubricated enough one night to say to him: "The end of *Ma Rainey* is a downer. You have to change that." Calmly, without any offense, he said, "No, it has to stay that way."

August waived his royalties the last month of our show, *Joe Turner*, and I am ashamed to say that month that I made more from that show than the playwright did.

One Friday, August and I were in the West Bank, and the playwright Romulus Linney, who is Laura Linney's father, kept going between his cast at a table, and we two who were sitting at the bar.

I knew who Romulus was: a prolific writer and a teacher at Yale. I had enjoyed his *The Sorrows of Frederick* Off-Broadway with Austin Pendelton. But he was no August.

Well, who was?

He kept leaning into August, who did not know him, and kept talking to us. When he walked away, I said: "He keeps pushing up against you, hoping some of your talent will rub off." Drink-fueled and cruel.

August always lived in a simple room in the Edison Hotel when he stayed in New York. Otherwise, the hill in Pittsburgh was his home—the place where so many of his plays were set. I'm glad to report that he was to finish his great quest: to write a play for every decade of the twentieth century, encompassing the black experience with plays like *Fences, Jitney, Two Trains Running, The Piano Lesson*, and others.

The only time I ever saw August get upset was when he was talking about his plays in general. He told me, "My plays are about my people. They are to be acted by them, and directed by them."

At the end of the night when we were done, August would slowly rise from the bar and check his pockets in that quiet way of his, to make sure he had his room key and his wallet. Then I would stand outside with him until I got him a cab so he could safely traverse the mean streets of Manhattan back to his hotel. After that, I would go upstairs to my apartment, which was now on the 33rd floor, where I could look all the way down 42nd Street from my balcony.

The last time I ever saw August, he was standing in front of the Edison Hotel on a summer's day in 2005. I went up to him and said, "Wait here."

It was between shows, and I knew the cigar shop down the block had a secret supply of Cubans. They sold me two, and I went back to August and we lit them up, and stood there shooting the breeze about my latest show with Jessica Lange and his latest play, *King*

Hedley II. He never mentioned his battle with liver cancer, which would sadly take him that October.

I hoped that summer day we would meet on that same street for many more years to come and smoke cigars from time to time. It was not important for him to talk about his illness. He was above that. There was more writing to do. Productions to see and guide. It made the news of his death that fall even more shocking to me.

And I know why. I've always had a special place in my heart for my drinking buddies.

***

The bad old days would continue through the 1990s until Mayor Rudy Giuliani with Police Commissioner Ray Kelly finally got the police out of their squad cars and put them back on the street walking a beat. There they acted as a visible deterrent to crime and found they preferred it to being in the cars. Now the merchants and restaurant owners knew them, and they rarely paid for a meal.

It also helped those of us who needed them in an emergency because they could easily be found.

Then things really started to change when investment came into Times Square, driving out the squalor of the porn shops and the decrepit movie houses. It was a slow process, but eventually "the good old, bad old days" became a thing of the past, which allowed Broadway to flourish into the modern era.

ACT TWO

NAME ABOVE THE TITLE

Alec Baldwin and Tennessee

WHEN THE STAR OF the show is a great inducement to buy tickets, their name is placed above the title.

There was a great buzz within our theatre months before we put the glass up on the marquee. We had bagged a production of *A Streetcar Named Desire* with Jessica Lange—in her Broadway debut—and Alec Baldwin, the newly minted, genuine movie star of *The Hunt for Red October*.

The Barrymore was, of course, the same theatre the show had originally played with Marlon Brando, Jessica Tandy, Karl Malden, and Hunter. There had been several productions of the play over the years, but none approached the Great White Way with the hype of this production, which was to be directed by Gregory Mosher.

It was a big show for Gregory because he was leaving the artistic director's position at Lincoln Center and going out on his own with this show. He clearly had aspirations to be a big, commercial director like Mike Nichols.

Meeting movie stars you've admired for years is always interesting. But working with them is downright revealing. Jessica Lange, a stunning beauty who was an acclaimed actress of the silver screen, was quiet and withdrawn.

Her acting on screen may have been beautiful and subdued, but there was a problem with her playing Blanche DuBois at the Barrymore: at first, her voice was too low; acting for the camera.

With Alec Baldwin, the tabloids kept writing about how he had turned down ten million to play Jack Ryan in the next two Tom Clancy movies. My impression was that this weighed heavily on Alec, only thirty-four, who only two or three years before had been hustling himself at casting calls, like any young actor.

The pressure was on to make this production something that would make people stop talking about Marlon Brando's Stanley Kowalski, a Mount Everest of modern acting.

They had cast the play wisely with Amy Madigan as Stella, Stanley Kowalski's wife. But as Stanley's best friend, Mitch—originally played by the grizzled character actor Karl Malden—they picked Tim Carhart, an odd choice. Tim was tall and handsome, probably best remembered for playing the rapist shot dead by Susan Sarandon in *Thelma and Louise*.

Unsurprisingly, the show opened to lukewarm reviews. I approached Hume Cronyn and his wife, Jessica Tandy, the original Blanche, after they saw the show.

"Would you like to go backstage?" I asked.

Hume quickly changed the subject.

He commented, "Jessica and I were discussing at intermission just how many years of our lives we had spent acting in the Barrymore Theatre," he said, somewhat nostalgically. He then added, "Seven years was the right amount."

Those seven years included his early success in *Elizabeth Rex*, her two years in *Streetcar*, their show together *Foxfire*, and others. There was a reverence in his voice when he spoke about the early *Streetcar*.

Many stories circled us about the great, original production: how Brando and Karl Malden would sit outside the stage door between matinee and evening shows and tell anyone who would listen that this was a pretty good play and you should come and see it.

Or how Brando broke his nose shadowboxing with a stagehand when things got a little too rough.

I asked Kim Hunter, the original Stella, about it later during another show she understudied, *An Ideal Husband*, at the Barrymore. According to her, the fake fight took place in the basement.

"Everyone had to lie and say it took place in the alley of the hotel next door because J.J. Shubert would have fired both of them for fighting in his theatre," she explained.

Brando did the evening's performance. After a scene with Jessica Tandy in which his nose started to bleed, he rubbed the blood on his sleeve.

"Swine," Jessica whispered as he passed her, walking off stage.

Brando then checked himself into a hospital as doctors straightened his nose the best they could. The producer, Irene Mayer

Selznick—Louie B.'s daughter and David O. Selznick's wife—visited Marlon in the hospital.

"Oh, Irene, I'm so sorry I broke my nose, but I'm so happy I won't have to do the show for two weeks," he said.

I took Cronyn and Tandy backstage to see the cast because that's what polite actors do.

The cast was thrilled to be within touching distance of the original Blanche DuBois. We knew Brando would never leave his home in Los Angeles to come and see the production, and Tennessee was gone.

Maria St. Just, the curator of Tennessee's estate, was around all the time. Alec Baldwin, a great mimic, would get on the house speakerphone and do a perfect rendition of her giving the cast notes.

"Now, cast, a little more energy tonight. And Alec, try not to sweat all over everything."

After two months, we had to deal with some unwanted drama when Tim Carhart became homesick for LA, or depressed, or perhaps both. He wanted out of the show. His understudy was given the role, an unknown actor named James Gandolfini.

The future *Sopranos* star was perfectly in tune with the role of Mitch. Big, brooding, everything the role demanded. Many agents saw him do the role, and soon after the run, he was off to the movies, and then, of course, the legendary HBO television show that cemented his position in the pantheons of the TV Gods.

But that was later. Right now, James was a quiet, introverted actor offstage, with a habit of being late for his cues onstage. You would hear this rumbling coming down the dressing room stairs, and you knew he was running to make his cue onstage.

He once got in a fight down in Greenwich Village, close to where he lived. He had to be bailed out of jail, and the female company manager called me up in a panic.

"Can you come with me to do this? I've never done something like this before," she said.

"And you assume I have!?" I replied.

My criminal record consisted of being arrested for peddling leather belts on a street corner in Manhattan without a permit. It was how I made some money as a young, struggling actor from time to time. One day, fifty of us peddlers were thrown in wagons and taken to a central holding cell.

With the next batch the wagon brought, a guy came in who had been selling kazoos.

He entered playing "When the Saints Go Marching In." We all sang the song at the top of our lungs. We were all soon released and given $20 tickets for our crimes.

I told her, "It's easy. You post bond at the courthouse and you won't even see James. He'll just be released from wherever they're holding him."

That night, James was most apologetic as he told the story of this "jerk" who was foolish enough to take him on with his massive shoulders. They were both drunk, of course.

That year, 1992, *Streetcar* had a very good softball team. Jimmy came out to play only once. I spoke to him about it years later in the

West Bank Cafe on 42nd Street, where he sat with other Soprano castmates, Steven Van Zandt and Robert Iller.

He told me he had been in Central Park all day out by the rocks, away from the game, smoking pot with Don Yesso, Alec Baldwin's understudy. When he came back and sat on our bench, he was secretly praying that I, the team's captain, would not put him in the game.

Well, the last inning came along and I sent Jimmy out to right field, wanting to play everyone who came out.

We were up three to two going into that last inning. We got two outs and then the other team got a man on base. Then one of their players hit a high fly to Jimmy in right. The ball took forever to come down and when it did, Jimmy reached his glove up and missed the ball by a mile. Both runs came home... and we lost the game.

When I asked Jimmy about it in the West Bank Cafe, he told me the whole story.

"After smoking pot all day, that ball looked like the planet Jupiter going over my head," Jimmy said.

An actress named Debbie, who was a member of the cast, dated Jimmy a couple of years later out in Los Angeles.

She said, "Jimmy would have two dinners, dessert, drink, and then do a little blow afterward."

He was a larger-than-life man, with many appetites indulged.

At the next table that night in the West Bank were six real wise guys from Brooklyn sitting by the three castmates. They used to like to go around with Tony Soprano, giving him all due re-spect, actor or not.

I remember Madonna coming up to me one intermission, saying, "The ushers tell me you're the manager. I'd like to meet Alec after the show."

I took her backstage, where three other women were also waiting to see Alec. Madonna said in her unmistakable style, "Well, I can see it must be 'take a number.'"

Alec had her in and out of his dressing room in three min-utes, because he was already taken: he was dating Kim Basinger and was soon to marry her. They had done a remake of *The Runaway,* Steve McQueen's earlier movie.

I took Kim out to her seat in the house at Alec's request and was stunned at her beauty. Early in my managing career, I had seen Catherine Deneuve enter the theatre and thought she was the most beautiful actress I had ever seen with her pale, almost white complexion. But Kim was every bit as beautiful, if not more so.

That summer, the couple took on the horse carriage drivers, demanding that they not be permitted to take out their horses if it was above 95 degrees. One day, about twenty drivers with their horses and cabs pulled in front of the Barrymore shouting in Irish brogues:

"We love our fecking horses! You blighter, Alec!"

Alec's response was to get on the shoulders of the biggest stagehand he could find, Kenny Tedesco, and wave at the dri-vers, which prompted much howling and hissing.

Alec and Kim eventually won their fight, and a law was enacted that the horses could not be taken out in extreme heat. Alec has always been a liberal activist for causes, and Kim, shy and reserved, went along with her man, but I got the feeling she was never completely comfortable about it when he said things like, "Let's go to Washington and stone (Republican) Henry Hyde to death" during a late-night talk show.

Kenny Tedesco, a real West Side hooligan, wasn't afraid to stand up with Alec either. Once, in the scene before he kneels and yells out the play's famous "Stella!", Alec pulled the door-knob off the set's door.

Unable to open it, he had to break the set's fourth wall, stepping around it, much to the audience's amusement.

Alec also complained about his hand because he hit the edge of a table during a scene, and it started to hurt. We replaced that corner of the table with foam padding, after which Kenny Tedesco said, "I don't know, Alec, we're going to have to do something about your acting."

Alec one day called me into his dressing room to complain about a lack of hot water at the end of the show. I had an engineer come by and the warm water seemed fine. Alex once went on David Letterman and was asked what was the difference between doing movies and Broadway.

"Well, in movies if you want a mountain," Alec began, "the next day there are two hundred guys building a mountain. I asked the manager for more hot water in my dressing room and he said,

'Katherine Hepburn never asked for more hot water. Dame Maggie Smith never asked for more hot water.'"

It is true I said that, but jokingly, of course!

I had my own six degrees of separation from Alec before our show. I had played football on Long Island against the Massapequa High School team, where Alec's father was the coach. I played at arch-rival East Meadow High.

Also, Alec was about five years younger than me, in age. At the barbecues we had in the Barrymore alley, between Saturday shows, Alec would walk around the party holding my one-year-old daughter Lucie.

On Letterman, I'm told Alec did a perfect imitation of me, always the great mimic. The next day I got a call from Gerry Schoenfeld, Chairman of the Board of Shubert, asking me: "Is there anything wrong with the hot water in the Barrymore?"

I told him, "The engineers and I have checked it, and it seems perfectly fine to us."

But there was something wrong. Something the engineers had hidden from me for years. The Barrymore and Longacre Theatre shared the same water heater. Now, you must understand that the heating, ventilation, plumbing, all that jazz was the engineer's department.

I once turned on the blowers when the engineer I called took forty-five minutes to get to the theatre, as the audience fanned themselves with their programs. I was told in no uncertain terms that if I ever did that again, I would be out of a job!

"No crossing union lines on Broadway, or else," I was warned.

Because of the shared water heater, if the show in the Longacre got out early and the entire cast took showers, then there was no hot water for the show finishing later. At the end of the three-hour-long Streetcar performance, there was no hot water.

This problem was not remedied until a complete renovation of the Longacre occurred years later when they got their own water heater. So Alec was right.

Alec made some members of the audience hot and wet in a much different way, I was soon to discover. I was at the back of the last row of the theatre and saw a beautiful thirty-year-old woman sitting in an aisle seat.

I picked up the "A" phone which was there behind a curtain so I could call the stage manager, and start the show.

I said teasingly to this stunning woman, "Five dollars to talk to Alec."

"I don't want to just talk to him," she said. "I want you to put me in the first row, so his beads of sweat hit me every time he moves."

It was the last time I ever joked that way to anyone.

As the run of the show dragged on into summer, Jessica Lange started to miss performances. Every time she was out, we at the front of the house would get slammed, as a third of the house demanded their money back.

Then, to make matters worse, Alec also started to take a show off now and then with the same result: enormous refunds.

One Thursday, Don Yesso, Alec's understudy, came up to the box office and ordered 20 tickets for that Sunday's performance.

"Uh-oh!" we all thought. Sure enough, Alec called in sick that Sunday and we got mobbed for refunds.

I saw Yesso backstage a few days afterward and said, "Boy, you and Alec better never rob a bank together."

The last days of August came, and the end of the run approached. Alec had taken to grading his performances and writing the results on his dressing room wall. Sometimes, he would grade himself in football terms like during the Actor's Fund performance. That is an extra performance for the Fund's charity. Alec wrote, "Baldwin fumbles twice inside the twenty, audience 20 and Baldwin 6, at the end of the first half."

His grading of himself moved up through the summer from sevens and eights to nines. It was true. As he gave up all that bull about not doing the Jack Ryan movies, he released himself to the words, emotions, and brilliance of Williams. He then completely, totally, became Stanley Kowalski. It was a marvel to behold, a performance of beauty and power.

My old acting teacher, Wynn Handman, would tell us in his class: "To do O'Neill, you have to become larger than life. But to do Williams, you have to surrender your heart to the words, the poetry, and let it break."

I met Tennessee twice, on two consecutive days. I was sent over to the Shubert Theatre to cover a special presentation. An organization was giving both Harold Pinter and Tennessee Williams special awards.

The future Nobel Prize winner Pinter, a tall, elegant man with thick horn-rimmed glasses, accepted his award with little fanfare.

Then Tennessee, short and hunched over, got up and thanked everyone, saying it was a very special time for him because his sister Rose was with him.

Rose had been institutionalized most of her life. She suffered from schizophrenia and had gone through a lobotomy fairly early in life. It was one of the veils of sorrow Tennessee carried with him all his days.

The next night, Tennessee Williams came by the Broadhurst where Peter Shaffer's *Amadeus* was playing. His seats were in the third row, not far from the pass door that led backstage.

I hurriedly went backstage and told anyone who would listen: "Tennessee Williams is in the house!"

A plan was made: anyone who wanted to meet him would stay in costume and I would take Tennessee through the pass door to greet the cast. After the curtain calls were done, after many ovations, I went down to Tennessee, who again was with his sister Rose, feeble, lost, but knowing she was with her brother who loved her.

To quote the ending of *The Glass Menagerie*, "Oh, Laura, Laura, I am more faithful than I intended to be. So, blow out your candles... and so...goodbye."

I told Tennessee the cast would be honored to meet them. All we had to do was walk through the pass door ten feet away and they would be there waiting for us.

He in his Southern gentleman's accent immediately said, not to be questioned: "Thank you, but my sister Rose and I must be going."

I went backstage where twenty actors in their grand 18th century costumes waited.

I told them Mr. Williams had decided to leave and got a huge collective groan from everyone like I was a thirty-year-old nitwit.

Perhaps he was shy about his sister, perhaps he didn't want to be fawned over, but then it all came clearer when I was told a story by Carlos Jimenez in the West Bank Cafe a couple of years later.

Carlos was a big, burly Spanish actor and a notorious, rabble-rousing, close-the-bar drunk. One summer, Carlos was a member of Tennessee's acting company in Key West. He had been thrown out of the place he was staying, for obvious reasons.

Tennessee told him, "Don't worry about it, baby. There's two weeks left in the season. Just come and stay with me."

"There was no 'come-on' in all of this," according to Carlos.

An old man, Tennessee just wanted someone to go drinking with at places like Sloppy Joe's on Duval Street. Every morning at 5:30am or 6am, no matter how late they had been out the night before, Carlos could hear Tennessee pounding away at the keys of his typewriter. He worked on revising his plays until the day he died.

One night when they had been out tying on a strong one, on the way home, Tennessee fell. Carlos picked him up.

"You know, baby, I suffer from terrible jealousy," Tennessee said.

Carlos then went, "You're Tennessee Williams. Who could you be jealous of?"

"Well, the Shaffer brothers don't do much for me," said Tennessee.

The Shaffer brothers! Like they were some terrible gang. These two identical twins in horn-rimmed glasses who wrote hit after hit in the seventies and eighties, like *Sleuth* and *Amadeus*. At the time, Tennessee could not keep plays like *Clothes for a Summer Hotel* open for a month. Jealous?

Well, the great Tennessee said he was.

But many of his words and phrases were—and still are—everyday lexicon, which is not something the Shaffer brothers can ever lay claim to. Such as in the following sweet little vignette.

There was a period when Tennessee had an apartment in Manhattan Plaza, where I lived.

An unknown actress was getting off an elevator when the doors closed on her, and her groceries fell all over the floor. Tennessee had been on the elevator, and ever the Southern gentleman, got off the car and helped her gather herself together.

She then said, not knowing who he was, "Thank you, I have always depended on the kindness of strangers."

Now how true that story is I do not know, but one story I do know about Manhattan Plaza and Tennessee that is true is the following: Mitch Douglas of ICM was Tennessee's last agent, after the legendary Audrey Wood had passed away.

He told me about one drunken afternoon when Tennessee just wanted to throw all of his papers down the incinerator shoot, including all his letters, correspondence, and unfinished plays. Mitch and Tennessee wrestled with each other over the papers.

"Just give them to me!" Mitch said.

It included letters from Lawrence Olivier to Tennessee about how he could make the movie more palatable for Vivien Leigh, who was then the great English actor's wife.

"No, it all had to go! Out! Throw it away! All away!" yelled Tennessee.

Thankfully, Mitch rescued a good amount of it, which he quipped was his "retirement savings." Within two years of the night Tennessee had come to see *Amadeus*, he was dead at 71.

Of all people, Marlon Brando said it the best: "Tennessee was close to death so many times that by the time it came, it was no more than a shave and a haircut."

Kathleen Turner

A TEN-THOUSAND-DOLLAR CARTIER WATCH was missing.

The victim was Kathleen Turner who swore blind she had left it on her dressing room table. Immediately she called Shubert's Chairman, Gerry Schoenfeld. He then called the police at the 18th Precinct. I was to meet two detectives at the stage door that afternoon.

Now, we knew Miss Turner liked her glass or two of wine after the show. I had met her at the Lyceum once during her *Body Heat* days, in which her brilliant performance and simmering sexuality had propelled her to stardom. She was now doing a star turn in *Indiscretions*, an English version of Jean Cocteau's *Les Enfants Terribles*. In the last decade or so, Kathleen had developed arthritis in her hands and had started to self-medicate with wine to help with the pain.

Which all made me wonder if the missing watch might eventually turn up. We all tried to stay calm when our dressers and cleaning ladies were questioned by detectives, along with anybody who had access to Kathleen's dressing room.

One cleaning lady said, "I know where it is."

She led the detectives to the star's dressing room and showed them where she had put the watch far in the back of Kathleen's make-up kit. She added, "I was afraid someone would take it, and that I would get blamed for it."

The caper was solved, and it made the cleaning lady in question look like Mother Teresa herself. But looks can be deceiving. She was eventually caught red-handed stealing items from another dressing room a year or two later.

Was she hiding the watch in the hope it would be unnoticed so she could take it another day? That's unknown, but the mystery was over.

However, there were times, an evening performance now and then, when Kathleen had a bit too much. There was obviously a lot of stress in her life. Her husband, Jay Weiss, was the owner of the Happy Land Social Club. He had leased the club to a man who committed arson because of a fight with his girlfriend, who worked at the club. As a result, eighty-seven innocent people had tragically lost their lives locked in by pad-locked doors as the blaze consumed all. It was the highest death toll in the history of New York since the Triangle Shirt Factory fire of 1911.

Though Jay was not found to be criminal in the case, there was the matter of $15 million compensation that was awarded to the victims. It was considered an outrage at the time that 87 Dominican lives were considered so cheap.

Sometimes, after a matinee, Kathleen was spotted going across the street to the Rum House between shows. The company manager and I went across to the bar and spoke to Rosie, the owner of the place. Rosie was a gentleman, a former Green Beret in Vietnam.

We asked him to politely cut her off at six o'clock, or we might not have a show. Kindly, gently, he did it without fail.

The show also starred a young Jude Law. At the beginning of the second act, he got out of a bathtub completely nude. I would see women almost throwing themselves at him after the show, but he seemed bored by it all. He was smitten with his girlfriend, Sadie Frost, with whom he eventually would have three children. He would break up with her to date actress Sienna Miller, among many others. At this writing, he now has six children!

Typically, for an English lad, his favorite post-show haunt was the same Rum House directly across the street from the theatre. I saw him there one night after the performance, and dragged him to O'Flaherty's, on Restaurant Row, on 46th Street.

He loved this Irish bar because they had a dart board, a game that's ingrained in the English DNA. He would take on everyone, winning most of his matches.

The rest of the cast consisted of Nixon as the daughter, Roger Rees (the original Nicholas Nickleby on Broadway) as the father, and Eileen Atkins, who left us midway through the run because she was diagnosed with cancer. I was delighted to see her again on Broadway twenty-five years later, playing with Jonathan Pryce in *Height of the Storm*.

The most amazing thing about the production was a set piece: a spiral staircase that the entire family spent literally hanging off in one scene.

One summer afternoon toward the end of the run, the temperature hit 102. The air-conditioning had failed, and the engineers were called in to fix it. They told me the problem was "substantial" and that they could do nothing about the situation until Monday.

"Monday!" I echoed.

It always amazed me that Shubert was a very "Monday to Friday" centralized operation, even though we always played weekends. This rendered the house unbearable, especially for both the audience and the actors under blazing stage lights.

We held a cast meeting between shows to see whether they would play that Saturday night without air-conditioning. They were within their rights and—more importantly—the boundary of union rules if they canceled.

"How's the house tonight?"

"We're sold out. It's a Saturday night."

Like soldiers in the Foreign Legion, they blankly exchanged glances, hot and still sweating.

The show was not a smash. Shubert was the producer. Losing a Saturday night's take would not make the powers that be happy.

I was asked to leave the room. I nervously paced up and down outside until I was called back inside a few tense minutes later.

"We'll do the show," said Roger Rees. "But do everything you can to cool off the place before tonight."

I think they did this to save my butt, more than anything else. The fact that both air compressors had gone out was not my fault, but the manager has ultimate responsibility. Blame always goes there first.

I gratefully thanked all five cast members. I told them I would do everything in my power to keep it as cool as possible.

Like an old sea captain, I kept the side doors open as long as I could. Then again, at intermission. Fortunately, the weather broke with a cool breeze running down the avenue. It was my very own miracle on 47th Street, with the blowers now pumping cool air into the full house, saving the show and myself.

A happy ending, the only happy ending the play ever had; it was a tragedy, with Kathleen Turner dying in the end.

I attended opening night of Kathleen's next starring role in *The Graduate,* in which she played the iconic Mrs. Robinson. Kathleen saw me at the party and invited me over to sit at her table. She was drinking club soda, sober as a judge. Soon after, she would do a brilliant Martha in *Who's Afraid of Virginia Woolf?* at the Longacre.

I remember how she would call me "Danny" in that deep, wonderful voice of hers, just like she did with Ned Racine in *Body Heat.*

Kathleen has continued working through the years, recently on television's *The Kominsky Method.* She has made a seamless transition to character actress, no easy feat.

She's done that because she brings her wonderful talent to all the roles she takes on.

Jude Law has become an international movie star, with the ability to do *Hamlet* on stage in the West End and on Broadway. I'm sure he still plays darts when he can.

Cynthia Nixon once played two roles on Broadway on the same night, namely in *The Real Thing* and the third act of *Hurly Burly*, both directed by Mike Nichols.

Then she became a household name in *Sex and the City*, the HBO success, which eventually led to a run for Governor of New York. Had she won, what a great loss that would have been for the theatre.

Finally, Roger Rees broke the hearts of all on Broadway when he passed away in 2015. His partner, Rick Elice, afterward said to me, "Roger always looked forward to going to the Barrymore because he knew you would be there to say hello and greet him."

What can one say?

It was the kindest thing anyone ever said to me.

Maggie Smith

I WALKED THROUGH THE iron door and strolled down the alley to the stage door, not knowing what awaited me. I noticed the radiator was loudly banging. Turning to Pete, my doorman, I said, "How long has this been...?" Then, startled, I turned to my right and saw Maggie Smith's face in livid contortion six inches from mine. Her fabulous career on stage and in films had made her an international star, and had led to her being dubbed a Dame of the British Empire by Queen Elizabeth. But she was far from ladylike during our first heated exchange.

"You're the manager?! This radiator has been banging for twenty minutes and it's driving me mad. I won't stay in the place if it goes on for another ten bloody minutes!" she shrieked. She returned to her dressing room which was right next to this radiator on the first floor and slammed the door.

I immediately called the engineers and had them run up to the Barrymore—and I do mean run—from 45th Street where their office was. They turned off the banging radiator and then drained the water from the iron sixty-year-old beast. Had Miss Smith carried out her threat to walk out on us, it would have been a major PR disaster and a death at the box office. All very bad for me.

I walked out onto the deck of the stage, which was the way through the pass door, up the side aisle to the stairs that led to my office. Suddenly, I heard: "There's my old friend."

It was Peter Shaffer, who remembered me from *Amadeus*. It was his new play, *Lettice and Lovage,* that had begun rehearsing that day onstage. I was never so happy to see a familiar face after my chewing out by Dame Maggie.

The play was about a tour guide who embellishes the history of a grand old manor house. I quickly learned the legendary actress Maggie Smith suffered from Graves' disease, which makes one overly sensitive to light and sound. A banging radiator is a bother to anyone, but it was amplified tenfold by this nasty disease.

Maggie and her rival, played by Margaret Tyzack, as the grand house's curator, constantly argued over her embellishment of history and downright lying. Eventually, they become friends and agree to do tours of other old buildings and decide that the show is more important than the real history—namely the truth.

They both deservedly won Tony Awards: Maggie for Best Actress and Margaret for Best Featured Actress that year. It was a huge success, running 286 performances. It was, therefore, very important for me to keep Dame Maggie happy and in residence by making sure the surrounding radiators never banged again!

***

As we neared the end of our nine-month run, Peter Shaffer became more and more livid over the fact that we had no luck finding a replacement for Maggie Smith, and therefore the show had to close.

The producers asked stars like Angela Lansbury and Julie Harris, among others, but no one wanted to follow Dame Maggie's Tony Award-winning performance.

A month before the end of the run, Faye Dunaway came by to see a matinee. I told her, "If you like, I can take you back to meet Dame Maggie after the show."

At the end of Act Two at the curtain call, Faye leaned down to pick up her purse at the same time as the lady in the seat next to her. The lady was quicker than her and hit Faye right on her nose with the zipper of her purse.

Bleeding profusely, I took Faye backstage and offered her a tissue, which she held against her wound as we waited for Dame Maggie to receive guests. It was then that I mentioned we were looking for a star to replace Dame Maggie.

"You would be wonderful in the part," I said, desperately wanting to keep working. I gave her our General Manager's number, who was Stewart Thompson. For four weeks, I did not hear a word. I simply felt nothing had come of it.

Then it was announced that Faye Dunaway would be playing the lead in the national tour of *Master Class*, another one of Stewart Thompson's shows. At least I had turned Faye onto him, and she had gotten work out of it.

Sadly, the end of December approached, and we closed the show.

Once, as I was walking down 47th Street, I ran into Bernie Jacobs, President of Shubert, as he was coming from a meeting at the Broadway League up the block. I said, "Boy, Dame Maggie is a handful, Mr. Jacobs. I walk on eggshells around her."

"Yes, but when she's onstage, are there any complaints at intermission, or ever?"

"No, Mr Jacobs, never."

"Then there."

Baryshnikov

I WAS SITTING IN my office on mid-afternoon as Act One of a matinee played to a packed house. The statement signed, the play up, I was listening to the basketball game and doing payroll. The announcer watched a player jump out of bounds and knock the ball back toward the court. "Boy, he really did a Baryshnikov on that play," he said.

Everyone understood what he meant by that. It was a beautiful, athletic, balletic leap that saved the ball for his team. It was then I thought I must get a picture with the person who was on the stage of my theatre: the very same Mikail Baryshnikov.

The cultural icon was playing the man who becomes a spider in Franz Kafka's *Metamorphosis*. Misha's movement in the role was brilliant, of course, which was good because he barely spoke twenty words of English. He had just finished the 1985 movie *White Nights* the year before, and the girls were crazy about him. We sold tickets like mad.

So, between performances, I got my little "celebrity" camera and went down to his dressing room.

"Picture?" I asked, holding up the camera.

"Picture?" Misha replied, nodding.

"Picture... with me?"

"Picture! Da. Da."

I had his dresser take the shot. This was the same dresser who loved telling the joke, because of the sometimes funky shape of a dancer's feet: "Oh, Misha, you're beautiful. But please put on your socks!"

Misha's sudden fame sort of overwhelmed him, especially when he had reduced some women to screaming like he was a rock star every night when he tried discreetly to exit the stage door.

This was the very man who, when asked in Europe what he thought of the women there, said: "English girls are great. They love to fuck!"

His girlfriends were well known from reports in the tabloids. The beautiful Jessica Lange, with whom he had a daughter, Shura. Then there was Tuesday Weld.

Something of an anomaly as a straight dancer, he was without doubt one of the great ballet dancers of the century and later a bona fide movie star because of the films *White Nights* and *The Turning Point*. The combination was deadly, plus he had that cute accent. It was like living with Mick Jagger in the place.

At the closing party, I remarked to him, "I just read that you're going to do another movie."

Interrupting, he spoke in broken English: "False alarm. False alarm. No movie."

Fifteen years later, I sat in front of him at a funeral service for the great Broadway dancer, Greg Mitchell. I had worked with Greg on

Song and Dance. Greg was only fifty-two when, tragically, he had a massive heart attack while dancing onstage in Washington with Baryshnikov. Greg passed a week later in a hospital there. Misha, who now spoke perfect English, gave me a wonderful hug.

"When we worked together," I said, "you barely spoke ten words of English. Now you're a regular chatterbox."

Laughing, he said, "I am a big hero to my kids now because I have a part on this TV show, *Sex and the City.*"

Obviously, his kids could care less about the ballet career of their father—regarded as the best in the world—who had danced his way from his native Latvia across the Soviet Union with the Kirov, then across the entire globe to New York.

"Sad about Greg," I said.

"Yes, tragedy. Great dancer. Good guy."

We all went to a reception afterward at a local restaurant called Nana's. What made the place special to all of us was that Greg had designed the interior, which resembled a street in a small town in Italy. Greg had crafted all the sconces and archways. It was just one example of the many things actors do when they are between gigs.

Two dozen of the best Broadway dancers were there who had worked with Greg. I watched as Misha humbly sat in a corner.

That basketball player had done a "Baryshnikov" indeed, fifteen years before.

Dame Judi Dench

MY STAGE DOORMAN PETER and I were anxiously awaiting a very royal return in 1999.

Dame Judi Dench, who had played a British Queen on more than a few occasions, was returning to the Barrymore. Her performance in David Hare's play *Amy's View* a couple of years previously was brilliant. Her name on the marquee was a sure thing, if ever there was one in this game.

Ed Bradley of CBS's iconic *60 Minutes* asked Dame Judi to do an interview for his show. Dame Judi agreed but said the only place she would agree to do the videotaping was on the stage of the Barrymore. As the theatre was dark, we were all called in: the stagehands, Peter, and myself, to do this special taping.

Dame Judi made her entrance in a low-key way. The greeting was warm all around.

She seemed almost embarrassed by the attention, with a slight blush as everybody welcomed her back. We had come to love Dame Judi for her dignified yet unpretentious persona. She was the word "class" personified.

The play *Amy's View* was about the twenty-year relationship between an actress mother and her troubled daughter played by Samantha Bond. Bond indeed! Because both of them appeared in several James Bond movies.

The reviews were quite good, which meant that this time there was no pissing contest between the press and playwright who had been up in arms the last time one of his plays had been savaged at the Barrymore.

Dame Judi had just won the Best Supporting Actress Oscar for playing Queen Elizabeth in the movie *Shakespeare in Love*. Amazing, because she was on screen for less than ten minutes.

She told me, "They really gave me the award for *Mrs. Brown*."

I remember her husband Michael came over from England for our opening night. The next night, Judi cautioned Michael that twenty to thirty people waited for her nightly at the stage door, and that she felt it was her obligation to sign their playbills and get photos with them since they had come to see her show.

"Please forgive me, it often takes some time," she told him.

Well, the next night was second press night: a jaded audience if there ever was one of distant critics, former press agents, and other people who had worked their way into a free ticket by knowing someone. Add to that, it was heavily raining. So, when Judi and Michael exited the stage door that night, there was one little old lady under an umbrella.

Judi went over to her, signed her program, and thanked her for coming. Then Michael and Judi got in her car to be driven home.

Michael paused for a second and with a wink delivered his line: "Well, that wasn't so bad."

You can be an Academy Award winner, the toast of Broadway in a new play, and still get your ego cut down with a wink.

Michael was not well with cancer and I was sad to hear of his passing a short time later, at the relatively young age of sixty-five.

The big stars who turned up at the show all wanted to get backstage to hobnob with Dame Judi. When Michelle Pfeiffer came by with my old friend Fisher Stevens, whom she was dating, she asked me, "What do we call her?"

I said, "Well, Dame Judi."

"You mean we actually call her by her title?" Michelle said.

"Unless you want to call her Dame Commander of the British Empire," I replied.

When Dame Judi received quests, people were always offered champagne on a tray carried by her charming, blond Scottish dresser, who was married to a friend of mine, Gabe Harris.

I always thought that a bit colonial and teased Dame Judi about it.

"I see the Scots are still working for the Brits," I quipped.

"She is just a wonderful dresser and friend," Judi said.

Judi's birthday came around during the run of the show and we had a special presentation on the stage of the theatre. Zoe Caldwell, another wonderful actress and Judi's friend, was the master of ceremonies and did a bit that went like this: "I kept going around and asking people who worked with her to tell me what they thought of Judi. They all said, 'Oh, yes, Dame Judi is marvelous.'

Then I probed deeper. Then they would say, 'She's wonderful, always wonderful.' I just wanted to find one person who would say, 'Dame Judi is great, *but...*'"

She paused dramatically, then said: "I could never get anyone to say, 'but.'"

I became good friends with Tate Donovan, who played the male lead in the show. In the summer, toward the end of the run, I was told by Tate to bring backstage America's sweetheart, Sandra Bullock. They just happened to be each other's former flame. Tate had told me they were going to dinner between Saturday shows.

That night, as I was walking into the stage door, I saw Tate walking back and forth like an angry tiger in a cage. I knew Tate well enough to ask him if everything was all right.

"She pissed me off," Tate said. "She told me she's made a hundred million in the last three years."

Sandra was box-office gold at this stage, no pun intended. Ah, the one that got away, I thought. And I never mentioned Sandra again to Tate.

When Ed Bradley's interview was done, we said goodbye to Dame Judi. She then walked down the alleyway and out the stage door of the Barrymore.

Peter put a small picture of her on the glass door that opened to his booth. Amazingly, it is still the only picture on the door and hangs there to this day.

Shortly after *Amy's View* closed, I was at another theatre filling in for the manager when word came down that my old boss and mentor, Alex Cohen, had died. He had produced over thirty plays on Broadway, the Tony Awards for many years, and multiple television specials for the Actor's Fund charity, like *Night of a Hundred Stars.*

There is a great tradition on Broadway called "Dimming of the Lights" when someone of prominence, like Alex, or Bob Fosse, or writers and actors too numerous to mention, passes. The marquee lights on all Broadway theatres at 8pm are turned off for a full minute.

This night, I received the memo that we would blacken the lights for the man who was my "rabbi" on the Broadway scene. I informed the house electrician who was to throw the breakers. We set our watches and at eight the lights of the marquee darkened. On a warm spring night, much of the crew stood on the street to see all the lights of Golden, the Plymouth, and the Imperial go out for a full minute.

I thought of the time when Alex saw the cot in the basement of the house on Locust Street that I was sleeping on during the production of *I Remember Mama* in Philadelphia. He immediately gave me a fifty-dollar weekly raise so I could pay my way and be with the rest of the guys in the house in my own proper room. I was happy on my cot, but the gesture was pure Alex. Kindness under the gruff and rough exterior.

The lights came back on, as one of the great traditions of Broadway again was practiced. Then we all moved into our theatres for that night's performances. As the old adage goes: The show must go on.

Madeline Kahn

AFTER WE WAVED GOODBYE to Alec Baldwin, Jessica Lange, and James Gandolfini, *The Sisters Rosensweig* was the next big production up at the Barrymore. It was moving from a successful run Off-Broadway at Lincoln Center.

It starred the wonderful Jane Alexander, with whom I had worked as a walk-on at the American Shakespeare Festival twenty years before. The cast also included the comedic genius Madeline Kahn, who had leaped to fame with her roles in the movies *Paper Moon, Blazing Saddles,* and *Young Frankenstein.*

It was written by Wendy Wasserstein, a feminist playwright who had built an amazing resume in less than ten years with the plays *Uncommon Women and Others, Isn't it Romantic,* and then the Pulitzer and Tony-winning *The Heidi Chronicles.*

Wendy had been on my radar ever since I ran into the Artistic Director of Playwrights Horizon, Andre Bishop, on 42nd Street. We had been in acting class together with Wynn Handman. Andre implored me to come and see Wendy's latest play, *The Heidi Chronicles.*

I always jumped at the chance of checking out promising work because Gerry Schoenfeld at Shubert had told me if I ever saw something wonderful to write him a note about it.

I was blown away by Wendy Wasserstein's play. Following the chain of command, I told Peter Entin what I thought, and then I wrote a note to Gerry Schoenfeld, who probably would have gone to see it anyway without my recommendation. But at any rate, the next week he saw the show and agreed to present it on Broadway.

The smash hit had put a feather in my cap, in Gerry's eyes. *The Sisters* was successful because Wendy's passion and comedy appealed across gender lines. It ran for a year and a half and went through two full casts.

One of the actors in the play was the comedian, Robert Klein. He was going through a divorce, and every other weekend, he had his young son with him. Robert was onstage much of the time, and his son was on his own, wandering the back of the house and backstage every Saturday afternoon.

Boredom soon set in, and the boy started throwing a ball against the side exit doors in the stage door alleyway, which the actors and the audience could clearly hear.

I was told about it and had to handle the delicate situation of a boy going through his parents' divorce when one of the parents was the star of my show. My solution was to befriend the boy. I would take him down to Broadway with his father's permission before the show for ice cream, or McDonald's.

"What would you like?" I'd ask.

"A cheeseburger and a chocolate malt."

"I've got to talk to you about something," I gently began. "You know how you like to throw your ball against the side of the theatre when your father's onstage?"

"Yeah?"

"The actors on stage and the audience can hear."

"So?"

"That upsets them. I tell you what: we're going to get a cable line up to your father's room and you can watch the baseball games instead. How about that?"

Mercifully, he was fine with that. There was a verbal question on the test the managers must take before they can become full members of the union. It goes something like this. Imagine Lauren Bacall says, "The show's drummer is throwing me off!"

What do you do?

"Well, have the conductor rehearse the drummer," was my first response.

"What if the conductor finds nothing wrong with his playing and Miss Bacall still says that he is throwing her off? Now remember, she is the headlining star of the show like she was in *Woman of the Year*. Without her, there is no show. What do you do?"

I thought for a second and said, "Get another drummer."

And that was, of course, the right answer. It is very important for all the managers—stage, company, and house—to keep their star happy. I could have said to Robert Klein, "Your son can't throw his ball against the wall of the theatre during the show." But that would have made no friends.

There is a ranking system in the Broadway Theatre: showmakers like Michael Bennett or Bob Fosse are at the top, followed by producers, then artistic directors, and then famous directors.

But equal to all the above are the stars of the show. And if they get unhappy with the theatre or theatre manager, it has a snowball effect and suddenly all the above are breathing down your neck.

With Robert's son, I was doing just what you should with Ms. Bacall and her drummer.

***

Jane Alexander threw a party that summer at her house upstate where she lived with her husband Ed Sherin, the late director best known in later life for his NBC series *Law & Order: Special Victims Unit* and the play *The Great White Hope*.

There was a wonderful natural pool next to the house that was fed by a mountain stream.

I saw my oldest daughter Chelsea, all of twelve, talking to Jane swimming in the pool's water.

I heard Jane say, "I've been in twelve movies and ten Broadway shows."

Chelsea said she also wanted to be an actress when she grew up. Later at the party, I got Jane alone and said, "You're supposed to tell her how incredibly hard it is... how few people become working actors, let alone stars like you."

It did no good. Chelsea, mind of her own, became an actress. She has many credits to her name on her IMDb page and appeared on television in *Grey's Anatomy* and in movies *The Equalizer, Night at the Museum,* and *Broken Memories,* but she now knows how hard the business is.

I have to say it was my privilege to work on a show that featured the great Madeline Kahn. Her comedic timing as Gorgeous Teitelbaum was always perfect, and she won the Tony for her fabulous performance. She played the role as she did always, almost detached from reality: loony, and yet so precise. She didn't suffer fools gladly.

So, it stunned me when, during the last week that she and Robert Klein were in the show, she stopped me in the alleyway of the Barrymore and asked me earnestly: "When Robert and I leave the show next week, will the show close?"

Now, I had learned that most actors look out at the house. If they see empty seats, they start to worry. This was not the case with *The Sisters.* There are so many things that go into the possibility of closing a show. Box office, yes. But also the will of the producers. It is ultimately their decision.

The cost of the production is another factor. Some shows are very expensive, even though they do not look it. Other shows like the musical *Chicago* are relatively inexpensive because the producer keeps the costs down.

They would replace Equity actors when they were up for an automatic raise. Then, after a few months, they would hire them back at the same rate they worked at before. The actors would agree to this because they know they can work a production contract for half the year, a good deal for a mature dancer.

Now, our ticket sales and advance were robust. It was obvious to all of us in management that with a new cast of stars coming in, like Linda Lavin and Tony Roberts, the show had months left to run.

I said to Madeline, "No, I think we're going to run for a time."

Madeline said, "I'm glad."

To this day, I don't know if she was serious or pulling my leg.

She passed too soon, five years later in 1999 at the age of fifty-six, robbing us of her comedic genius and fun-loving heart.

One last thing about Madeline Kahn was that on her dressing room door, she placed a framed cartoon from *The New Yorker*. It was a drawing of a king and a knight standing on a castle wall. As they looked out, they saw thousands of warriors on horseback.

The caption read: "Genghis Khan! I thought we were expecting Madeline Kahn!"

Paul McCartney

THE THEATRES I COVERED were dark in the summer of 1989. Peter Entin called me up and told me to go back to the Lyceum and handle a special event: a concert with Paul McCartney and Wings. The members of this band on the run were staying stationary for an entire month to rehearse, then doing a small concert, before going on the road for a national tour.

"It's all very hush, hush," according to Entin. "No publicity, no talking about it, no nothing."

Has there ever been bigger stars in Western culture than the miracle called *The Beatles?*

My mind drifted back to the days in the late seventies when I used to ride my bike all over the city. Central Park was my destination mostly as I drifted past the horse-drawn carriages and the many joggers. I would ride off the main road and cut through where "Strawberry Fields" now stands. I would often pass John Lennon and Yoko sitting on a bench in mid-morning.

One day, I simply waved at them and they waved back.

That became a tradition whenever I would see them. I guess they simply knew me as the "bike rider." I never approached them or said a word. What a tragedy it was when a crazed fan shot Lennon down. The heart of the city broke that day.

Suddenly, I was roused from my daydream as three large tractor-trailers pulled up in front of the Lyceum stage door. They were loaded with couches for the band, televisions, rugs, mirrors, telephones, and anything else you could imagine that was electronic. Apparently, people like Mr. McCartney go nowhere quietly, even if it is all "hush-hush." They set up the dressing rooms and the stage with their instruments. When they finally came to the stage that afternoon, after tuning up, they played two of their new songs that I did not know. I was in my office at the back of the orchestra, with the door slightly open, doing payroll.

Then suddenly McCartney broke into an oldie but goodie: *Money Can't Buy Me Love.*

I threw my pencil in the air and started dancing like a madman. This was the music my brother and I grew up on and adored. The Beatles, the wonderful Beatles, who changed the world of pop music.

"Can't buy me love... no, money can't buy me love..."

Looking onstage at him and his left-handed guitar, you felt you were seeing what he loved most. It also felt like you were looking at something this man was born to do.

Every day Paul and Wings rehearsed, there was the most wonderful vegetarian spread put out for lunch by a half dozen chefs. The lovely Linda McCarthy herself was there every day. One day when lunch had just begun, I found myself standing across the serving table from McCartney and had the nerve to ask him, "What is your favorite Beatles song? 'Blackbird'? 'Hey, Jude'?"

Not looking up from his plate, he said: "Well, the Beatles were yesterday. I prefer to look to the future and think of the music I'm yet to make. Always look forward, I say."

I've always thought perhaps his answer was in what he said with the word "Yesterday."

One day, his wife Linda poked her head in my office. Accompanied by her assistant, she said to me: "So, this is the manager's office?"

"Not really. The real office is upstairs, where we keep Shubert's archives."

"What's it like?" she asked, sounding genuinely interested.

"Well, let's all go and see." We went up the lobby elevator to the floor above the balcony.

Opening the metal gate, I introduced Linda to the two archivists and pointed out J.J. Shubert's chair on display in a corner. It was a garish thing made of gold leaf and velvet, and at the end of each armrest, there was a dragon holding the world in its mouth. Linda sat in the chair. "He must have been a king," she mused.

"He was," I said, "of the American Theatre."

I showed her Daniel Frohman's peephole, the Lyceum's builder and first owner. From this vantage point, he could open a small door and see his actress girlfriends performing on stage. Paul now had come onstage and had begun tuning up for the afternoon session.

Linda saw him, and began shouting, "Paul! Paul!"

He looked around as if the voice must have been coming from heaven. His voice lessened as he said, "Linda, where are you?"

The month passed quickly as I heard the new music McCartney spoke of—"Band on the Run"—and the rest of his cracking tunes, with my office door slightly open.

On the day of the freebie concert, a long line that ran down the block had formed outside. Ron Delsner, the promoter of the show and the band's tour to follow, asked me to take Paul out a window and onto the marquee, which was under renovation, in order for him to wave at the waiting crowd. Looking around, I said, "It's just too dangerous to have the star walking around over all the pipes and beams up there." Amazingly, Delsner agreed.

The concert, simply put, was madness. We opened the doors of the theatre and the masses rushed in. People ran up to the balcony and opened the fire doors of the theatre to allow others in. They all went running down the five flights of the fire escape to open the pass doors and let numerous friends in. They then ran up to the balcony and packed in.

The one usher up there came down and told me what was happening. I went up there to see the balcony packed with people standing in the aisles. Seeing as there were no tickets, it was impossible to check who had entered the theatre legally, and who had not. The only thing to do was to start the show as fast as possible.

Also, the band had been sending people to the stage door and getting their friends in that way. Rock 'n' roll indeed!

I caught a little blond girl backstage wandering about and asked what she was doing.

She claimed to be Ralph Lauren's daughter. "We're friends of Paul," she said with that blank stare that all the models in his ads have. I simply replied, "Yes, you are!"

Then I turned to the stage manager. "It's best to get it going and hope a fire marshal doesn't come by." But it turned out to be all of another fifteen minutes later before the "boys were ready to play." The concert went on for almost three hours.

The audience left delighted: the largest audience the Lyceum ever had. They departed slowly into the night. The next day, the trailer trucks were outside to take the televisions, the chairs, and the instruments away. Paul came downstairs from his dressing room on the way out with the lovely Linda. The entire stage crew and I awaited him to say our goodbyes.

"So long, lads," McCartney said, and then he was off.

The next day I was finishing up paperwork in my office, in the dark and lonely Lyceum, and I remembered a favor that had slipped my mind in the middle of all the madness: the deli owner across the street had begged me for a signed picture of McCartney. There was a stack of pictures of Paul on my desk that the press agent had left behind from the media conference the day before the performance.

I said, "Oh well," and cheekily signed one: "Best wishes, Paul McCartney."

I went over and gave it to the deli owner, who was so grateful he made me a free sandwich.

Every two years or so I would go into that deli on 46th Street, next to the Equity building, and there it would be, hanging on the wall. Ten years passed, and the deli owner was still the same, but the picture was gone. I went to him and said, "There used to be a picture of Paul McCartney on the wall."

"It hangs in my son's room now," he said. Then he looked at me as if I might be familiar. "But people tell me that is not his real signature!"

***

Linda died several years later, and I wrote McCartney a letter of condolence. A neighbor in Montclair, New Jersey, was Paul's press agent in America, so it was simple to get my letter to him. I mentioned the story of when Linda's voice seemingly descended on him from the heavens.

I also told him of my only brother's sudden death in a car crash in Kentucky on Halloween in 1996. In the middle of the afternoon, a lady lost control of her new truck and crossed the yellow line, striking him head-on. Her son had committed suicide the year before.

Was she high on tranquilizers? Depressed and in a state of anxiety?

I found out you could not legally ask those questions. The accident happened only minutes after he got off his disc jockey shift at three PM in the afternoon at a local radio station.

Of course, I wrote, he always loved the Beatles. Two weeks later, I received this in the mail:

Dear Dan,

Thanks for your letter of condolence and the lovely stories that accompanied it. It was good to hear your reminiscences of our lovely Linda and I am glad you are keeping them close to your heart. My sympathies go out to you on the loss of your brother Chris—Boy, life ain't easy!—but I am glad to see that like me and the kids, you are remembering the good times and drawing strength from them.

With very best wishes,

Paul

I'm reminded of the lyrics to a certain song whenever I see Paul's letter to me:

"Oh, I believe in yesterday..."

The Shady Ladies

I WORKED ON FIFTY Broadways shows. What comes to mind when I think of them is not determined by the success of the show, or the fame of its stars. Instead, my memories are all about my interactions with those who worked on those shows.

The first show out of those fifty productions that comes to mind—for difficult reasons I will soon share—is *An Ideal Husband* by the Irish icon Oscar Wilde, who wrote only a few plays in his lifetime. He might not have been a prolific fiction writer, with only one short novel to his name, but his opinion of himself was grand.

Entering America, a customs agent had asked him if he had anything to declare.

"Only my genius," was Wilde's response.

One day he ran into his literary agent in the street. The agent asked Wilde if he had worked that day. Wilde's response was, "Yes, I moved a comma."

This production of *An Ideal Husband* was directed by Peter Hall, who had also directed *Amadeus* from my early days as a manager. Sir Peter always said to me, "Why are American theatres kept so cold?"

Wearing a warm scarf in the last row of the orchestra, he would sit covered from the neck up.

The production received wonderful reviews, and we settled in for a nice, long run. I became good friends with the English stage actor David Yelland, who played the husband. We played golf near my home in New Jersey several times.

But things dramatically turned into a nightmare on Halloween in 1996. We had just gotten word that my wife's beloved grandmother had died at the grand old age of ninety-four. We were off to Alabama for her funeral the next day. Later that night at around 8:30pm I got a call from my sister-in-law, Lou Ann.

In a flood tears of she told me my brother had been killed in a head-on car crash at 3:15 pm in Elizabethtown, Kentucky. He was five minutes off his shift at his radio station when a woman lost control of her new truck and crossed over the yellow line and smashed into him.

Chris and I had been very close. We had just spoken a few days before because the New York Yankees had won the World Series. I was destroyed. He was only forty-three, cut down in the prime of his life.

He had left behind an eleven-year-old son, Joshua.

After the funeral, I remember sitting in a restaurant as a family across the room sang "Happy Birthday" to someone at a nearby table. Cruelly, it would have been my brother's birthday forty-fourth the very next day.

I was heartbroken, but the show must go on. When I returned from the two funerals, the cast of *An Ideal Husband*—every single one of them—was kind to me. All offered their condolences, something I will never forget. In the theatre, we care about the person you are, not how big a star you are.

The next show at the Barrymore was called *The Life*. It was a gritty depiction of street life in New York in the late seventies and early eighties. It had original songs by Cy Coleman who had a string of hits on Broadway such as *Sweet Charity, Barnum,* and *City of Angels.*

The score was brilliant with songs like "The Oldest Profession," sung by Lillias White, who won the Tony For her performance. A beautiful string of chorus girls played the shady ladies led by Pam Issacs, Felicia Finley, Judine Richard, Stephanie Michels, and Bellamy Young.

Chuck Cooper led an ensemble of hustlers, pimps, and thieves.

After one show, I found a middle-aged Black woman who was crying at the back of the house.

"Are you alright?" I asked.

"You know, life sometimes isn't so easy for some people," she whispered.

The fact that the show was graphic in its depiction of street life and the brutality of the relationship between pimps and prostitutes was its flaw. In a Broadway musical, there are many things you can depict, but cruelty to women, to where the audience is cringing, as when Chuck Cooper's character slammed Pam Issac's head into the back of a bar rendering her bloody, pushes the limit.

The book was by David Neuman, one of the writers of *Bonnie and Clyde,* and Ira Gasman, who became a wonderful friend to me. A classy Brit, Michael Blakemore, was the director. I always thought he was an odd choice for a show that depicted such a raw slice of Americana.

The show was a little confused also in that the costumes with high platform shoes and big pimp hats were right out of the '70s, yet the show claimed to be set in the '80s.

There was a line about someone finding two tickets to *Cats.* I mentioned to the director and writers that *Cats* opened in 1983, so that is the earliest date our show could be. The writers and director immediately cut the line.

If ever there is a rule backstage during the performance, it is this: don't stare. If the cast is changing, look away, and keep your head down. I had to fire a stage doorman for refusing to do so.

There was a scene in which after dancing in a strip club, Bellamy Young, who was to find television stardom on *Scandal,* takes her top off.

She was facing upstage, so all the audience saw was her bare back. Well, this doorman would go into the wings far upstage to watch her do so.

I told him, "You've got to cut that out! She sees you out of the corner of her eye and has complained to me about it. That's not your job, anyway. You're supposed to stay by the stage door."

He refused to stop, even after I had warned him. So he was fired.

When the Tony nominations were announced, we were nominated for Best Musical, Best Score, and several other awards. There was a rumor at the time that the producer of *Titanic*—our chief competition for those awards—had taken the out-of-town Tony voters on a party boat on the Hudson River for drinks and dinner. That producer had allegedly whispered in their ears that, "*The Life* will never play your theatres."

Meaning the sordid depiction of prostitution would not fly in Kansas City, St. Louis, and Salt Lake City.

On Tony night, *Titanic* sailed home. It won everything except the acting awards for Chuck Cooper and Lillias White.

Our show had struggled through that spring and with no boost from major awards, the producers decided to close *The Life* early that summer. Roger Berlind, a wonderful gentleman of the theatre, had a rough season with two good shows not doing the business required to run. Those shows were *Steel Pier* and *The Life*. He decided not to put additional money in and that was that.

***

One summer night three St. Louis Cardinals baseball players came by the theatre: McGwire (who was well on his way to hitting 70 home runs that summer), Gary Gaetti (another slugger), and Tom Lampkin (a back-up catcher).

Mark, a mountain of a man, asked me if he could meet Felicia Finley after the show. I saw Felicia backstage and told her, "You should marry him for three years, get ten million in the settlement. Then your current boyfriend and I get a million each, and you keep the rest and we ride off into the sunset happy." I was completely joking, of course.

Felicia—a Tony nominee a little time later for *The Wedding Singer*—laughed at that. She was a beautiful blond from New Orleans whose two southern religious aunts had told her, "You're going to hell for playing a whore on Broadway!"

I took the baseball players backstage and thought nothing more of it. Over a decade later, Felicia was playing the lead in *Mama Mia* and I was covering *Phantom* at the Majestic when we ran into each other at John's Bar on 44th Street after our shows.

She told me, "Mark and I dated for four years."

In the end, they drifted apart because she would not give up Broadway for him. Now she was happily married to a musician. But I was astounded that the little silly joke I suggested almost came true.

***

Speaking of baseball, or more correctly, softball, there is a great tradition called The Broadway Show League. It started in 1955 with casts of Broadway shows going up to Central Park to play each other in softball games while also having a picnic. It became a formal league a year later and has played consistently on Thursdays in the park ever since.

Show against show, union team against union team. For some, it's serious competition. For others, it's a social event to meet old friends from past shows.

I once saw Al Pacino in a blazer and dress pants play third base for the Actor's Studio team. I saw John Lithgow, all six foot four of him, make a triple play, catching a line drive as he was playing first, stepping on the bag for two outs, and then running to second to wait for the chorus girl who, when the ball was hit, ran all the way home, only to have to return to second where John gently tagged her for the third out. I'm told, though I did not see it, that George C. Scott once threw a no-hitter in a slow-pitch softball game. The odd thing is Mr. Scott would look in from the mound and shake off the catcher as if he was giving signs. The game is slow-pitch softball, so the only two pitches are slow or slower. The League has always been a great way for the cast and crew to get to know each other.

Out there on the field, a star can be a goat, and an usher a home run-hitting hero. I was commissioner of the League for six years and was interviewed on National Public Radio about it. When asked, I commented, "Well, there are a lot of gray areas in an actor's life. You didn't get the part because you're an inch too tall. You didn't get the part because you dance too well. You're perfect for this part, but it's been cast with a star. But a softball score is not one of those areas. If *Les Mis* beats *Phantom*, 3 to 2, well, then, they're just better than them."

The result of that can be playing to win. Even cheating. One certain team would actually keep stagehands on payroll as they went and played softball. Oh, and they were *really* good ballplayers. They got caught by management and there was hell to pay.

I remember the heartbreak of many a playoff loss. A bunch of actors, or theatre folk, all would like to imagine they're playing in the Major Leagues. Then after a day or so, the pain goes away and we start dreaming about next year.

Oh, what a team we would have had if the show had continued to run. The League has played consistently since 1955. The year 2020 was the first spring and summer there were no games because of COVID-19. I couldn't wait for the balls to fly again on a beautiful Thursday in Central Park.

Sondheim and Stoppard

SOMETIMES WRITERS OR COMPOSERS of magnitude deserve the honor of "name above the title."

Perhaps the word "genius" is thrown about a bit too much in the world of the theatre. But there are two people I have worked with who most certainly deserve to be considered for the distinction: Stephen Sondheim and Tom Stoppard.

Putting It Together was a review of Stephen Sondheim songs from his many musicals. It starred the wonderful Carol Burnett, Bronson Pinchot, and George Hearn, my old friend.

Often, I would take guests backstage to see Miss Burnett, who was one of the leads alongside Jack Lemmon in Billy Wilder's *The Front Page*. Carol would always ask their names and without fail, as they left, she would thank each one for coming to the show, remembering everyone's name. Amazing and classy. After a while, she told the producers she would prefer to do seven shows a week, as the strain of eight was a bit much for her.

The producers hired Kathy Lee Gifford from the morning television show *Kathy and Regis* to help carry the load. She was married to the football great Frank Gifford of the New York Giants, who was a boyhood hero.

Kathy played the show one night a week, Tuesday. Without fail, her husband Frank joined her in coming to the theatre. At around eight o'clock, just as his wife was about to go on stage, he would ask me to go across the street to the Rum House and have a drink with him. Being easily recognizable, he preferred not to drink alone. These were the few minutes he had before the start of the show to knock back a drink to help unwind. Once the show began, he had to watch his wife's performance in its entirety.

I would say, "I would love to Frank, but I have to start the show, and then count the box office, and then do my rounds."

The happy couple began throwing us a party after every performance of Kathy's at B. Smith's down the block, and I wound up having many a drink with my hero, Frank.

Carol clearly needed her night off, but it's not widely known that Kathy almost did not do the show. She would go over to Steven Sondheim's townhouse to go over all her songs. She read one lyric and stood up and said, "I'm sorry, I can't do the show."

"I don't understand," Sondheim said.

"This lyric, I can't do it,"

"What lyric?" said Sondheim.

"This lyric, 'God damn them'."

"In heaven's name, why not?"

"I can't take the Lord's name in vain," she said.

Kathy Lee is a highly devout Christian, an evangelical.

"Well, what could you say?" Steve asked.

"I suppose I could say, 'Fuck them!'"

"You could? Then let's do that," Sondheim reportedly said. Kathy did the show without taking the Almighty's name in vain.

Ten years later another Sondheim show played the Barrymore, a revival of *Company*. John Doyle was the director. The conceit of the show was similar to his production of *Sweeney Todd*. In Doyle's *Company*, all the actors also played instruments, save for the leading man, Bobby, played by Raul Esparza.

A revival, yes, but an actor I knew asked me: "Does the great Stephen Sondheim ever come by the theatre?"

"Well, it's his show. He's there all the time, every day. What do you expect him to do? Just sit in his townhouse?"

Early in the run, I was called to the back of the house by an usher who told me: "Mr. Landon, there's an old man videotaping the show at the back of the theatre."

I saw in the back row who the old man was. Sondheim! He was videotaping his own show, and the reason was this. It was Jessica Wright's last performance as Amy, the crazy bride who sings "I'm Not Getting Married Today." Jessica had taken over for Heather Laws, who had given birth to a baby. Heather had started in the show at the Cincinnati Playhouse, where it originated. The Equity rules state when an actress gives birth, she gets her part back in the show after she delivers the child.

Heather's rendering of the role was very good, playing it as neurotic and breathless as possible in the best fashion of a musical comedy character actress. Jessica Wright was different. A beautiful ingenue, she internalized the psychosis and Sondheim loved her interpretation. That's why he was taping her last performance.

Though taping the show is against the rules, what was I to say or do? He was infringing his own copyright, and he was Stephen Sondheim. What to say to the living legend?

As he was walking out of the theatre after the performance, I figured it out. I said, "Goodnight, Stephen."

***

Raul Esparza, a widely regarded stage actor who is perhaps best known to non-theatregoers for his role in *Law & Order: Special Victims Unit*, had married his high school sweetheart, Michelle Perez. They both were Cubans from Miami. But then Raul came out as bisexual in a New York Times profile piece on him in 2006. The couple divorced two years later.

One night Raul was way too drunk to stumble in on his wife. So, he called the company manager and asked to crash at his West Side apartment. But here's the kicker: the company manager had two Dalmatians. The sweetness of the sweat coming off Raul's face was irresistible to them at six in the morning, and Raul woke up with the two dogs licking his face.

But he ended up with an undeserved licking at the Tonys. At the end of the show's run, the week after the Tony Awards, Sondheim was very happy. An Australian theatre company in Sydney was doing *Company* and had invited him to come and see it, all expenses paid. He was looking forward to the journey when he ran into Raul backstage. Raul, who had won all the other awards for his performance as "Bobby," had lost the Tony to David Hyde Pierce in *Curtains*.

Raul told Sondheim, "It broke my heart that I didn't win the Tony for this."

Sondheim replied, "Oh, I'm not over losing the Tony for Best Musical to *The Music Man* when I had *West Side Story* fifty years ago."

***

There was—feel free to groan—no *stopping* Tom Stoppard in the West End, but Broadway was a different kettle of fish, especially when you've got a genius only willing to cut three lines from a three-hour production.

The Real Thing was a revival of Stoppard's, which starred Steven Dillane and Jennifer Elle. Like Sondheim, Tom was around all the time, a delightful, brilliant man. I had worked briefly on the original production at the Plymouth Theatre when it starred Jeremy Irons, Glenn Close, and Christine Baranski. I will never forget Christine's line in answer to her prying husband as to why she took her diaphragm on a business trip: "I didn't take it. It just went with me."

David Leveaux was the director of the new production. It became very important to him that his production looked nothing like the original, which was directed by Mike Nichols. Mike was called in to see our production and said, "It looked fine."

There was a problem though: he didn't remember a single thing about his production!

David, Stoppard, and Mike asked me to join them for a drink after the show since I was there during the original.

This prestigious meeting was held at a table in the corner of the Rum House, the same dive bar across from the Barrymore that Kathleen Turner would go to after her matinee performances. We went through every scene that I remembered from the previous show. In the end, it was decided that there were few similarities between the two presentations, which made David Leveaux happy.

The show was as successful as the first. Again, Stoppard's tale about the mystery of attraction was a hit.

Eleven years later, in 2011, another Stoppard revival came to the Barrymore. Considered one of Stoppard's most brilliant plays, *Arcadia* took place in different centuries. One set of scenes was about a group of researchers going through the records of another time. Their interest was the happenings in an English manor house during the visit of Lord Byron. The other scenes dealt with the actual happenings in 1809. There was one set for both eras. It had a great cast of actors: Billy Crudup, Raul Esparza (again), Margaret Colin, and Meryl Streep's daughter, Grace Gummer. It was a play about philosophy, quantum physics, dimensions, the meaning of time, little things like that.

It had brilliant passages like: "People were talking about the end of physics. Relativity and quantum looked as if they were going to clean out the whole problem between them. A theory of everything. But they only explained the very big and the very small. The universe, the elementary particles. The ordinary-sized stuff that is our lives, the things people write poetry about—clouds—daffodils—waterfalls—what happens in a cup of coffee when the cream goes in—those things are full of mystery, as mysterious as the heavens were to the Greeks."

Genius, indeed. But we still needed what's called "putting on a show" to get bums in seats. The running time of three hours certainly didn't help. Tom sat there for a month of rehearsals and cut all of three lines. We stumbled along for 108 performances. At the end of the run, Tom declared, "I'm never coming back to Broadway again."

Of course, he has been back since. As I recently told an aspiring Irish playwright who approached me for guidance on his first production: "Yes, Broadway is crass, commercial, even cruel, but the public takes to what it does. In a strange way, it's one of Broadway's saving graces. You sell the tickets and pay your bills, or you close. What 'art' people will see and value in five hundred years, like Shakespeare, is unknown. But a gross at the box office is reality."

Arcadia was a brilliant play; I wish it could have run for years, like *Joe Turner*. Sadly, it did not. My wife has always said to me she would leave me for Tom in a minute, with his wavy long hair, deep-set eyes, and slight Eastern European accent. So seductive was his writing to her.

David Mamet

ANOTHER GOLIATH OF MODERN theatre is a man from Chicago.

David Mamet burst on the scene in the late seventies with plays like *Sexual Perversity in Chicago* and *American Buffalo,* the first Broadway play I ever paid full price to see. He later cemented his reputation as one of the greatest playwrights of his or any other generation with *Oleanna, Glengarry Glen Ross,* and *Speed the Plow.*

He was praised for turning his often-used profanity into a strange and beautiful theatrical poetry with such lines as:

"To teach these people, you have to kill them."

"Tell the truth. It's the easiest thing to remember."

"They're only words... unless they're true."

"Put. Down. The coffee. Coffee is only for closers."

"As you know, first prize is a Cadillac Eldorado. Guess what second place is? A set of steak knives. Third place is, you're fired!"

And about life: "My vision of perfect happiness is a healthy family, peace between nations, and all the critics dead."

Lastly: "I grew up in a tough neighborhood. We used to say you can get more with a gun and a kind word than just a kind word."

This prolific writer of plays, movies, books, and essays was a real tough guy, with a love of martial arts to boot. I'm sorry, a tough, tough Jew, from Chicago. He would understand my saying that because words are only words... unless they're true.

A production of his play *November* was my first show with Mamet; it featured Nathan Lane as the President of the United States in a scenario in which the polls are telling him there is no way he will win re-election. So, on the way out, he decides to sell pardons. Illegal, yes, but who cares?

The cast alongside Lane—Laurie Metcalf, Dylan Baker, and others—played the comedy of the farce brilliantly. Mamet was there all of three days, listening to the show from behind a box curtain. After that, he felt it was enough. He pronounced the show ready for its opening. Mamet took the cast to Angus McIndoe's bar and told them, "You are not to change a word of my play."

Nathan Lane and director Joe Mantello had been fighting. Mamet pulled them both aside and said, "You two need to get along. Otherwise..." He then went back to Los Angeles.

The press agent was a wonderful Black woman named Irene Gandy, a character beyond compare, who said to me: "Well, all the critics have to say is Nathan Lane is funny and we'll run."

Nathan had become a huge Broadway star by virtue of his brilliant performances in *Guys and Dolls* and *The Producers*, among many others. The critics did hail Nathan as being very funny, and we were off to the races with a ten-month run.

The show was produced by Jeffrey Richards, who had been the press agent at the American Place Theatre when I worked there. He had hooked up with Mamet as his producer after a very successful revival of *Glengarry Glen Ross* that starred Alan Alda and Liev Schreiber. He has remained Mamet's producer until this day for all his presentations on Broadway.

Nathan liked the theatre on the cold side (my department) and I kept it that way for most of the run save for one miserably cold, rainy April matinee when the audience came into the theatre shivering like drowned cats.

Nathan saw me between acts and shouted, "Turn the air conditioning off!"

The stage manager double-checked. "Excuse me, Nathan, did you say turn it OFF?"

"Yes," he said. His wish was our command.

One summer day at around 1:30 pm I saw Nathan running down 47th Street late for his matinee call—and I do mean running. I could imagine the stage managers saying to him, "Oh, Nathan, you're late by a minute, and we're putting your understudy on." To which I would have said, "And giving back half the house?? That's sheer and utter madness." Nathan had gone to St. Peter's Prep in Jersey City. I imagined you could take the boy out of St. Peter's, but you can't take the Prep out of the boy. If he was late, the Fathers would be mad at him.

I became good friends with Nathan's oldest brother, Dan. After our Sunday matinees in the warm months, there was always a limousine outside to take Nathan to his summer home in the Hamptons.

I said to Dan, "With all the success Nathan's had, he must have a wonderful view of the water out there."

"No, he lives behind a movie theatre in town. It's all about going to the parties," Dan said.

Although he was wonderful in the movies *Mousetrap* and *La Cage aux Folles,* there was a story a short time later about Harvey Weinstein pushing Nathan against the wall at one of those parties and threatening to end Nathan's career, to which Nathan replied: "You can't threaten me. I don't have a movie career."

Speed the Plow was my next show with Mamet; again, it was produced by Jeffrey Richards. It was to star Jeremy Piven from the HBO show *Entourage*, Raul Esparza, my star from *Company,* and Elizabeth Moss from *Mad Men* in the part Madonna originally played on Broadway. I remember when the Material Girl would exit the stage door, bedlam would ensue with screaming fans running alongside her limo down 45th Street banging on the windows. Our show opened to critical acclaim, and it looked for all the world that we would settle in for our run of several months.

There was, however, trouble in paradise. Raul Esparza grabbed me one day backstage and said, "You know what Jeremy said?" He didn't wait for me to ask. "He said, 'I know you weren't feeling well yesterday, Raul, because the audience wasn't laughing at any of your lines.'"

Elizabeth Moss also told me she wasn't a fan of our star, to say the least.

But Jeremy seemed born to play one of these Hollywood hustlers. To give credit where credit is due, all three actors in the show were wonderful in their roles.

We were all gutted when Jeremy Piven told the producers he could no longer continue in the show because of what he called "mercury poisoning" from eating a steady diet of sushi.

The real problem was this: he loved the clubs. "He's staying out partying until late in the night. Correction, late into the morning," one of his drivers told me.

He clearly wanted to bask in the limelight. He was, after all, in the very successful run of the television show *Entourage*, which had brought him fame and fortune to the tune of three million a year. Mix that with the grind of doing eight shows a week in a demanding play and you can easily find a breakdown in spirit, in health.

But he should have known better. His parents ran an acting school in Chicago. The very basic environment in the theatre where the work of the great plays is studied and performed. Where actors learn the craft and one would hope a love of the discipline required to perform on stages anywhere, let alone on Broadway.

Later that night the stage manager told me: "Jeffrey Richards is considering closing the show rather than go on without a star in the leading role."

***

Enter stage left: David Mamet. He leaped into action and asked one of his best friends, William H. Macy, to step in and save the day. Macy agreed but asked for four weeks of rehearsal before going on. Piven's understudy, Jordan Lage, went on in the role and was better than fine. He was downright good. But Richards panicked and asked Norbert Leo Butz, another Broadway star, from such shows as *Dirty Rotten Scoundrels,* to come in for a month until Macy was ready. Norbert said he needed a week before he went on. When he did, he still wasn't ready and carried a book onstage, a copy of the script, which was understandable.

But never was an audience so angry with me. They, after all, were paying full price to see an actor reading the play (who wasn't Al Pacino) and many wanted their money back.

One day Leo was in a terrible car accident, with his whole family in the car. Thankfully, no one was seriously hurt, but the car was totaled. Nevertheless, like the trouper Leo was, he made it into work and did the show.

Jeffrey Richards never had Jeremy Piven examined by his own doctor, which he had the right to do. I always thought—and this is my opinion alone—that Jeffrey did not want to alienate a star because he made a living from stars performing in his productions, which now on Broadway is almost mandatory, especially in plays.

But he could've done with a fighter in his corner. Someone like one of the tough gal characters played by Lucy Liu—the star of *Charlie's Angels* and *Kill Bill*—who came by to see the show in our last weeks.

I went up to her in the lobby and introduced myself as the manager. After chatting a minute, I asked her a question: "How much did you practice before you shot the sword scene in the snowy garden against Uma Thurman in *Kill Bill*?" Without missing a beat, she said: "Not enough. I lost, didn't I?"

The nightmare experience, thankfully, didn't turn Mamet off our theatre. The final Mamet play to grace the Barrymore during my time was *Race* in 2009, starring Kerry Washington, James Spader, David Allen Grier, and Richard Thomas.

Every show on Broadway goes through a fire inspection before it opens. Ranking members of the fire department from the ladder house around the corner on 48th and 8th Avenue come by, check the fire exits, the scenery, its flammability, etc. Mamet was directing this play himself, saying: "It was a play about race and the lies we tell each other about the subject."

We were nearing the end of the fire inspection and were waiting for the cast and Mamet to stop rehearsal. Then we could lower the asbestos fire curtain, the final part of the inspection. Mamet kept rehearsing the same fifteen-line part of the script that was laced with profanity, which, of course, he was famous for. After going through the same fifteen lines for the fifth time, he came onstage, realizing the obvious. He turned to the firefighter waiting in the wings and said, "I'm sorry, fellows, for assaulting your virgin ears." To which Lieutenant Tracy, the chief inspector, said, "We've heard those words before."

Two final Mamet stories.

Marilyn Sokol, a funny, weird comedian and actress, came by the show in its last weeks.

She knew me from around town and had done a production of *Sexual Perversity* which Mamet had acted in with her. She said, "I told him I really liked two jokes in the show. Would he mind if I used them in my stand-up act? He said, 'Fine, just pay me a hundred dollars for them.' I never paid him and now he won't speak to me."

At our closing party, I asked Mamet, "Crazy Marilyn Sokol says you won't talk to her because she never paid you the hundred dollars she owed you for two jokes."

"It was a hundred twenty dollars, and can you imagine what that would be now with interest thirty years later?"

Now, I thought, that's a true commercial playwright.

***

Mamet returned to New York the last week of the run to see his friend, William H. Macy, do the lead in *Speed the Plow*.

While the audience was entering before the start of the play, Mamet and I were standing by the back of the house, next to the curtains Katherine Hepburn had made us put up during the run of *The West Side Waltz*.

She said it was because the light of the opening doors during matinees bothered her. We were casually standing when he said this about his play about Hollywood hustlers: "I couldn't write this play now. I'm one of these guys."

Left:
My Lyceum ushers.
The ones who asked Whoopi Goldberg, "Do you share?"

Below:
Whoopi and me,
many years later.

Above:

The great Baryshnikov. At the time of his Broadway debut in *Metamorphosis*, he spoke maybe twenty words of English.

Below:

Opening night of *Joe Turner's Come and Gone*.
L-R: Spike Lee, August Wilson,
New York Knick Benard King and wife.

Above:
The wonderful Madeline Kahn and my daughter Chelsea.
"Since I'm leaving the show, will it close next week?"

Right:
The wall of Alec Baldwin's
dressing room during
Streetcar where he
graded his performances.

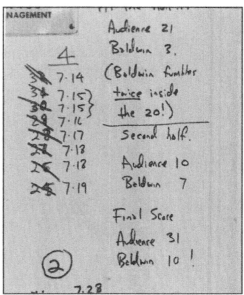

Left:
John Lithgow
waiting to bat in the
Broadway Show League
the day he had an
unassisted triple play.

Below:
The girls from *The Life* on closing night.
L-R: Judine Richard, me, Felicia Finley, Katy Grunfell.

Above:
Me and Robert De Niro.
When I asked will he ever
come back to Broadway?
"Never say never."

Right:
Engine 54.
Never Missed a Performance.

Above:
Rob McClure's dressing room during *Chaplin*.

Below:
Broadway Alley BBQ.
L-R: Cherry Jones (*Doubt*), me,
Sarah Paulson (*The Glass Menagerie*).

ACT THREE

THE BIG MOUSE AND THE SORROW OF 9/11

Serene

SERENE. THAT'S THE WORD I think of when I think of that perfect September day.

It was my day off. I saw the attack on television. The first plane hit the World Trade Center, an accident perhaps. But then, with the second plane, another word was uttered: terrorism.

After trying to reach my wife on her cell phone—no luck—I drove to the supermarket. My mother, who was seventeen at the end of World War II in Europe, impressed upon me how there was no food at the end of that war. Bombing, fighting, death everywhere, but also no food.

I was coming out of the market with a cart full of groceries when an F-22 fighter at about two thousand feet cracked across the sky above the parking lot, heading for New York City.

With all the cell phones out, I did not know my wife had decided to leave Manhattan by climbing on a ferry to cross the river. There she saw the second tower crumble. The terror of the moment must have been unimaginable.

Slowly, the ferry moved away from the Manhattan dock and made its way to Weehawken across the Hudson River. My wife told me a woman on board heard her dilemma of not being able to return to our home in Montclair fifteen miles away. The woman, who lived in Weehawken, offered to drive my wife back to our home. The woman checked that her husband had picked up her children, and then did just what she promised. She drove through roadblocks on Route 3 to my home, not knowing if she could return to her own.

Another man on the ferry joined up with them covered in dust. He had been on the fourteenth floor of Building One when the first plane struck. He had descended the stairs and escaped. However, the dust cloud from the falling building enveloped him with grey ash.

They all arrived in the alley of my home, and after a grateful hug with my wife and her newfound friends, I offered to drive the man home to where he lived in Ridgewood.

On the way there, we heard on the radio there was concern that chemical weapons had been delivered with the strike of the planes. My heart rose in my throat. It was absurd, pure fear. The explosion of the jet fuel would have destroyed any biological or chemical agent, but such was the volume of fear on that day.

Two days later, all the Shubert managers were called into a security meeting. The FBI was there and said they considered the Broadway theatres to be a prime next target. One said, "If a bomb goes off in a trash can on Times Square, we believe that your business would be virtually shut down. Americans are not used to this."

Nevertheless, we returned and opened the theatres. From that day on, all bags were to be checked by a security force headed by a local Midtown North sergeant, Andy Lopez.

It is the nature of getting an audience into a Broadway theatre just before curtain that you can be a little overwhelmed. In that case, I would jump in and check bags. One day, a man opened his bag, and I looked in to see a nine-millimeter pistol.

"Oh," the man said as he showed me his police badge from his back pocket. Many an explicative ran through my head, which I kept to myself.

***

Charles Busch—or Charlie, as we called him—had made a name for himself Off-Broadway in drag. He would play the female lead in his outrageous shows such as *Vampire Lesbians of Sodom, Red Scare on Sunset, Boulevard du Paris*, and others. He told me the most he ever made in a week downtown was around three hundred for writing the show and playing the lead.

Well, he sent his latest play to Lynne Meadow, the Artistic Director of Manhattan Theatre Club. Soon she called Charlie in. Charlie told me he was so excited, thinking he finally would be playing a starring role on Broadway.

During the meeting, Lynne Meadow said to him: "You know, Charlie, I think we would have something here with your play if we put a real actress in the lead."

Charlie shrugged and agreed. His play was going to be on Broadway, after all. She proceeded to cast Linda Lavin in the role and directed the play herself.

The reviews were marvelous. The show would go on to run two years, an ideal New York comedy for the era of the 9/11 attacks. Charlie stopped in my office one day and looked at the many photos I had put up on the wall. One was of Tom Stoppard, Jennifer Ehle, and myself, the one I previously mentioned. Charlie said, "Oh, look, Tom Stoppard. I wonder where he is now?"

I said in reply, "You'll see, Charlie. After six months of Broadway royalties, anywhere he wants to be." We figured, as successful as *The Allergist's Wife* was, that by the end of our 777-performance run, and the national tour that followed, that Charlie Busch made two million, easy.

***

It was a strange time in New York. Everyone seemed to know someone who had died on 9/11. The West Bank Cafe was closed for renovations, so I adopted Mr. Bigg's bar on Tenth Avenue. I heard many a story there of people lost in the Trade Center and other stories about guys in their thirties who had breakdowns and completely stopped working.

There was an NYFD Rescue Squad down 43rd Street between 9th and 10th that had lost many members downtown. Bigg's was their bar, too. It was a karaoke bar, and between drinks, we heard many a song murdered, which contrasted with the actual murders that had happened there because the place had been the club-house of the feared Irish gang "the Westies" in the early 80s.

Scott, the bar's owner, always hired good-looking bartenders. One was Mandy Gosling, Ryan Gosling's sister. Another was Sunni, a portrait artist from Chicago. Another was Enders, a doctor's daughter and dancer from Mississippi. They drew the young men of the neighborhood like flies. Meanwhile, I had a running hit in the theatre. Michele Lee, one of the stars of *Allergist's Wife*, made it her duty to go to the many funerals of the eleven men lost from the firehouse around the corner. She became their friend, their sister. That does not mean that sometimes their interactions weren't a little blue.

Al Schwartz, one of those firemen, who sometimes doubled as a stagehand on the work crews that do take-ins and take-outs, once said to me, "Ask her what's under a fireman's kilt?"

"You want me to ask my star, Michelle Lee, a question like that? I won't do it."

"Just do it," Al said. So, I did.

Without a moment's hesitation, Michelle said, "His big fire-hose!"

That's how we survived that time. With tears and humor. Those who lived through those days in New York will never forget them. And though there is pain in those memories, there is also pride and courage. At the firehouse around the corner, which has served Broadway for decades, on one truck they have the phrase, "Never missed a performance." They never have, even on the fateful day of September 11 when eleven of them were climbing the tower to fight the fire when it came down.

Battalion Chief Ed Geraghty was their CO and one of the nicest men I ever knew. There were never any problems with him that you couldn't quickly fix. They were all heroes on that fateful day.

"Only the good die young," as my grandmother Laura used to say. Only the good.

Presidents and Kings

DAME MAGGIE WAS NOT the only royalty to grace Broadway. Presidents, prime ministers, and real royalty like Prince Ranier and Princess Grace regularly attended. John Kennedy Jr., American royalty, walked into the Barrymore with his wife two weeks before his fatal plane crash on his way to the Kennedy compound that ill-fated summer night.

So here is a tale or two about the heads of state that I crossed paths with.

Former President Gerald Ford and his wife Betty came by to see *Amadeus*, the last Peter Shaffer play I had worked on, shortly after he had lost the election to Jimmy Carter. The Secret Service set him up to meet me and I escorted Mr. and Mrs. Ford to the top of the orchestra aisle. There I handed him over to my usher, Mary Jo Cashen, and she escorted them to their seats, giving Mrs. and Mr. Ford a program. The former president promptly took out a pen and signed it, and handed it back to Mary Joe. She kept that program.

She then handed Ford another program, saying to someone famous for tripping while coming off of Air Force One and other gaffes, "No, Mr. President, this one is for you."

The US Secret Service paled in comparison to its Israeli counterpart, the Mossad. They were the most serious and menacing people I ever encountered during my time on Broadway, full stop.

One day, they told me that their Foreign Minister, Avigdor Lieberman, would be coming by to see *The Curious Incident of the Dog in the Nighttime*. I had dealt with the Israelis before and had met both Yitzhak Rabin and Simon Peres.

I took the head of the detail into the theatre and we saw where the minister's seats were.

It was determined that the best way to get him into the theatre was for me to open the side door to the theatre alleyway right to where his seats were. So, I stood there holding the gate open, allowing Mr. Lieberman to avoid the crowds in the lobby. Now, Mr. Lieberman was highly conservative, a controversial individual. At about 7:45pm, with the audience filing into the theatre, Mr. Lieberman's three cars pulled up about seventy feet east of the Barrymore. The minister and about ten—count 'em, ten—Mossad agents got out of the cars. They drew their Uzis and 9mm handguns and walked toward the theatre.

The only thought in my head was that if a car backfired, they would shoot anything standing, turning me into Swiss cheese.

We got the minister to his seat, and I went back to the front lobby, breathing a sigh of relief.

But the best story of all Israeli encounters occurred a few years earlier when Benjamin Netanyahu attended a show with his wife and one security guard. Mr. Netanyahu was not in power at this time but would be again shortly. At intermission, his security guard came up to me and said, "I'm not enjoying this. He says I can go out if it is all right with you." I didn't know what to say. Then, I said, "Why don't you just stay in the lobby?"

The former and future Prime Minister of Israel sat there alone with his wife. During the many times the Barrymore was dark, I was assigned to other theatres in the Shubert chain. Once I was assigned to the Ambassador Theatre where *Ain't Misbehavin'* was playing. It was a revival with the original cast: Nell Carter, Ken Page, and Andre De Shields. Secret Service came by in the afternoon and told me former President Jimmy Carter and his wife, Rosa, were going to see the show that night. The theatre's prop man and I met with the head of the former president's detail.

We told him there was a gunshot in the show. "It takes place in the 'Joint is Jumpin' number when Ken Page points a starter pistol at the ceiling and shoots it."

"Yeah, sure. Everyone's a comedian," the agent replied.

"No, we mean it. There's a gunshot in the show."

At any rate, it was discussed how to take Mr. Carter backstage, seeing as the whole cast wanted to meet him. Because of the odd configuration of the Ambassador, a circular theatre, I told them the easiest way to take him backstage was up the four steps used in the show that led from the orchestra floor to the stage. It was agreed I would do so.

After the final bows, I went down to the former president and led him and his wife onto the stage while the audience filed out. When he hit the top step, the entire house exploded into the loudest ovation I have ever heard for a dignitary or politician. No one, but no one, denies the inherent goodness of Mr. Carter with his many acts of charity so well known.

When we walked offstage into the wings, I turned to the former president and said, "Well, that hand wasn't for me."

To which he replied, "They must be Democrats."

The Big Mouse Comes to Town

IT HAD BEEN OUR fervent wish, all of us who worked on Broadway, that large amounts of corporate money would enter the scene to help save the neighborhood from the blight of porn shops and crime.

Though the streets of midtown still could be pretty rough from time to time in the mid-nineties, there was a burst of light on the horizon. After being elected New York City Mayor in 1994, Rudy Giuliani and Police Commissioner William Bratton instituted a "broken windows theory," which prosecuted petty crimes like panhandling, loitering, and harassment.

The police would find as time passed that this was more to their liking since they were now known to the shopkeepers, the restaurant owners, hot dog vendors, and the rest. Again, they were the cops on the corners and visible deterrents to crime.

It was around this time that I received a call from the two men who were staffing the New Amsterdam Theatre, which Disney had purchased and was in the process of renovating.

The New Amsterdam, named after the early Dutch city, had been built in 1903, just like the Lyceum. It housed the *Ziegfeld's Follies* through the early century but fell on hard times as a legitimate house during the Great Depression and was forced to operate as a movie theatre after 1937. It stayed that way until 1965, when it closed down. Over the ensuing years, it became in terrible need of repair.

***

I met with John Petrafesa, who had been the number two man with the international union IATSE (International Alliance of Theatrical Stage Employees), and Disney's Vice President, Skip Malone. My old boss, Alex Cohen, had recommended me to them. John intended to negotiate separate labor deals apart from the League of New York Theatres and Producers. Skip was along for the ride and was learning.

I was told they were not happy about the return on investment from their first Broadway show, *Beauty and the Beast*. Alan Menken and Howard Ashman's movie had been turned into a Broadway Musical. It was running, but not making huge profits.

Coincidentally, Menken and I used to live in the same building at Manhattan Plaza. Our daughters were born about the same time, which meant we would have what I called "Stroller Wars," since both of ours would barely fit on the elevator at the same time.

This was when his first musical hit *Little Shop of Horrors* had just opened Off-Broadway at the Orpheum Theater downtown on 3rd Avenue.

John and Skip Malone asked me, "What would you do first in opening this new theatre?"

I told them, "You have to use Local #1, the stagehands, or else your scenery might not make it to the theatre through their picket line."

Also, I said that I would use #751 ticket sellers, who know how to sell out a 1700-seat house. Petrafesa was a little miffed at that. He was hired to get new agreements apart from the old work rules. Regardless, they offered me the job. All I wanted was a year-long contract like I had at the Barrymore.

After all, I had a young family: a twelve-year-old daughter named Chelsea, a nine-year-old son named Philip, and a four-year-old daughter named Lucie. I wanted some protection for them and myself. I feared Michael Eisner, the chairman of the company, would come in and ask me a question I would flub and he would shout, "Get this guy out!"

That was downright paranoia, but still, I just wanted a contract like I had at the Barrymore.

They did call me once more to offer me the job. Again, I said, "Fine, but I want that contract."

That was the end of any discussion about the position.

A year later, they opened the beautifully renovated New Amsterdam, restoring it to the glory of the *Ziegfeld Follies* days. The first two things they did was hire Local #1 union stagehands under a different contract where the house heads—props, electrics, and carpentry—made more money than in the League's agreement, with a modification of some of the work rules.

They also hired union treasurers. So, in the end, they did exactly the two things I had urged them to do.

Their first attraction was *The Lion King*, which was a roaring artistic and financial success. The Big Mouse was at the Broadway table for good.

Beauty and the Beast would go on to run thirteen years on Broadway and would gross a phenomenal $1.7 billion worldwide, changing Disney's perception of the money that could be made in legitimate theatre.

Julie Taymor brilliantly directed *The Lion King*. The puppets in the show moved exactly like the many animals from the wild African plains.

A decade later, she would direct *Spider-Man: Turn Off the Dark*. They kept spending and spending on the show until the budget was rumored to cross $75 million. Feeling it was all out of control, the producers fired Julie.

She sued them and received a settlement of $1 million.

An actor I knew in *The Lion King* calculated that with all the companies of the show around the world, Julie must have made at least $11 million in royalties in that one year.

I said to the company manager of another musical mega-hit on Broadway, "Seventy-five million is enormous, but movies can cost that and way more. One day your show with flying monkeys will gross two billion, won't it?"

"Oh, we've grossed way over two billion, on our way to what we figure will be at least four billion."

That show, *Wicked,* was produced for eleven million dollars. I often wonder how different my management career—and my bank balance—would have been had I moved over to Disney, because there was a highway in the sky with them when it came to opportunity. I worked for the six same men in the pecking order at Shubert my whole life.

I was happy at the Barrymore, knowing everyone on 47th Street. I would wind up spending twenty-eight years at that same theatre, for which I'm grateful. One, however, always wonders what the road not taken would have brought.

A decade later, I would run into the actress, Charlotte d'Amboise, backstage at the Ambassador where I was filling in on the long-running *Chicago.* Charlotte was playing Roxy for a three-month run for the third or fourth time.

We had known each other for twenty years by then, having worked together on *Song and Dance.*

I said to Charlotte, "Don't tell anyone how long we've known each other."

She turned to me and said, "That just means we survived in this crazy business, Dan."

Amen, to that.

Jessica Lange

SHE CAME FROM CLOQUET, Minnesota. You could take the sexy bombshell out of the countryside but, despite global fame, you couldn't take the country out of someone who was essentially a farm girl at heart.

After traipsing across America and living in Paris with her first husband, Paco Grande, Jessica Lange headed to the Big Apple after their split. Fortune as a model soon followed and then she was discovered by Dino De Laurentis, who put her in the lead in his new version of *King Kong*.

Amazingly, her acting career survived that, and she next appeared in *The Postman Always Rings Twice* with Jack Nicholson. He said of her, "She's a fawn crossed with a Buick."

I'm sure he meant those 1950s Buicks made of the same steel as World War II tanks. She was then charming the world in *Tootsie*, and won the Academy Award for Best Supporting Actress, followed by awards for *Frances* and *Blue Sky*.

She was a freak of nature: a supermodel who could truly act, beautiful beyond compare, with the sensitivity of that fawn, the tough skin of that Buick. She attracted famous men: Bob Fosse, Baryshnikov (whom she had a daughter with), and then the renowned playwright turned actor Sam Shepard, whom I had briefly known during my time at the American Place Theatre.

A production of *The Glass Menagerie* brought Jessica Lange back to the Barrymore in 2005. It was the first time she had been on Broadway since *A Streetcar Named Desire* with Alec Baldwin. Lange was a strange choice for Amanda, the part Tennessee Williams patterned after his mother. There was a line in the play stating that she had not had a date in the twenty years since her husband had left her. One wondered... had all the men in the world gone blind?

Also, there were problems in rehearsal with Dallas Roberts, who had been cast to play Tom, the Tennessee part, in this piece of memory theatre. Jessica and Dallas did not see eye to eye about the play. Dallas put his head in her lap during a rehearsal, which lent an oedipal touch. She found that wrong, or that's what I was told. It resulted in a shouting match, which ended in Dallas getting canned.

In a desperate scramble, the movie star Christian Slater was hired to replace Dallas only four days before opening. Christian was not a regular on Broadway. He was the son of casting director Mary Joe Slater and had risen to fame through movies like *Heathers* and *True Romance*. Living the fast life in Hollywood, he had run into addiction problems.

Nevertheless, he remained an upbeat guy. Fun to have around the theatre. He was delighted to be doing a Broadway show with Jessica Lange, Sarah Paulson, and Josh Lucas.

Again, David Leveaux was the director.

After his daily afternoon rehearsal, Christian would go across the street to The Rum House bar and would engage whatever stranger was sitting next to him into running his lines. I imagine quite a few tourists from the Midwest had a great tale to tell when they returned home to Ohio and Iowa.

The understudy Joey Collins began performances in the role and was quite good, but he wasn't a movie star like Christian. Broadway had become a place for such stars to work because producers believed they sold tickets. Christian opened in the role in front of the critics who found the production lacking.

Still, because of the star power of the two leads, we sold tickets, and we were bound to do the entire run. I remember after the show, after all the guests had come backstage and left, Jessica would sit on the fire escape and enjoy a cigarette alone. Then she got in the car the company provided her, and was driven home.

Sam Sheppard would come by now and then. My impression was always that Sam was a real cowboy in his heart and spirit. But it hit me that he had changed ever so slightly since fame grabbed a hold of him. Although a legendary playwriting career now joined an outstanding movie career, the poet of American alienation had become more distant, even paranoid.

He became upset one time when someone asked to take a photo with him and his son by Jessica. He refused the request and was angry about it. Trying to protect his son, I suppose.

As an actor, his natural style in such movies as *Days of Heaven* and *The Right Stuff* was unmistakable. But he was an even better playwright; his writing was unforgettable in *Buried Child* and *Fool for Love* with their depiction of the loneliness and the vastness of our country.

An actor friend of mine ran into Sam at the Improv in Los Angeles. They sat talking all night, and after closing time came, they got another bottle and went up to Jessica's house in the Hollywood Hills. At four in the morning, after making too much noise, Jessica came down the stairs and threw them both out. My friend headed home to Santa Monica, while Sam went out to a cabin he kept in the desert to sleep it off.

Through the summer, we would have barbeques in the theatre's alley. We would set up a grill and invite people from other theatres and shows. The whole cast would attend, sitting on the fire escape to eat, drink beer, and smoke cigarettes. That part of the theatre was open air with a grating blocking our alley from the parking lot next door.

Cherry Jones, who was starring in *Doubt*, and was a friend of Sarah Paulson, would always be there. Quoting the Rolling Stones song "Miss You," I said to Christian at one such barbecue: "Hey, I've got some Puerto Rican girls coming by, and they're just dying to meet you."

Christian went, "Oh, yeah, what are their names?"

He landed himself in a bit of trouble toward the middle of our run. He got into a fight with a girl he was dating. "She wanted to go out and score some cocaine," according to him, while he simply wanted to go upstairs to his apartment to bed.

A fifty-two-year-old woman was passing by and Christian, for some reason, went over and grabbed her backside. He and his date, both intoxicated according to eyewitnesses (duh!), stood on the corner of the block and continued to fight. The butt-grabbed woman called the cops. In two minutes flat, the cops were there and arrested Christian. Of course, the incident was splashed across all the tabloids.

Here's the real kicker: Christian had priors from his partying days. Thankfully, he was released and was at the theatre the next day, but we all shook our heads. It seemed like just another small black cloud over our little show.

We had a tradition on the show: after a two-show day, the stage manager would call me into her office as I was on my way out of the theatre, and she would offer me a small shot of Patron Tequila. During the last show of our play's run on a Sunday, I was called in during the second act.

I sat there with the company manager and the stage manager and we started on the tequila early.

Christian came through and declined to join us.

Jessica came through next, looked at us as if we were three sad sacks, paused for a second, and said to us: "If I had to do this show Tuesday, I would kill myself."

I ran into her sitting on the fire escape that last week of performances and said to her, "You might be disappointed with the way this second time on Broadway went, but they say the third time is a charm." She shook her head and said, "I don't know."

I got the strong impression she would never return. However, in a couple of years, she was back on Broadway playing Mary Tyrone in *Long Day's Journey into Night*, which was a critical smash. She even won the Tony for Best Actress. The third time was the charm, indeed.

She has remained one of America's great actresses in everything she does.

Four years later, in 2009, she split with Sam Sheppard. He died of ALS in 2017 in Kentucky. They lived the lives of movie stars, but they were never that. He always remained the rugged, handsome cowboy, and she the beautiful farm girl who broke the heart of every local boy when she left Cloquet to conquer the world.

Al Pacino and Other Characters

WE DIDN'T KNOW WHAT to expect when it was announced that Al Pacino was going to do a semi-rehearsed reading of Oscar Wilde's play *Salome* at my theatre with a stellar cast that included Dianne Wiest, Marisa Tomei, and David Strathairn. Though the cast read the first act, in the second act, they put down their scripts and the play went into motion.

Regardless, we were certainly going to sell tickets at full price.

Al told me, "It is all right if I do a play now. I did three movies last year."

When I found out that Pacino's fee for a movie was $10 million, I completely understood.

Marisa Tomei had me post two ushers by the stage looking out for the red lights of recording devices. She did not want anyone videotaping her dance of the seven veils and posting it online, because every fourth or fifth show she would take her top off. She also demanded two security guards be hired for her, simply because she wanted to keep up with Al, who had two security men.

Pacino was another actor, like Bobby De Niro, who feared the public and crowds. Often, when he attended any of our shows in the past, I would find him behind the box curtains at intermission, hiding and waiting until the lights went down and the second act began.

He said to me, "The problem is when I go out to get coffee and a newspaper in the morning I'm always running into someone who goes, 'Oh, Al Pacino, I love you!' A total stranger who thinks we should hang out together."

A true method actor, before the play, Pacino would go onstage and do lines in a whisper to the set, the house, everything, while getting into the character of King Herod.

When I told Al we broke the house record for gross attendance for a play in one week, he simply said: "That's nice."

I would stand across the street and watch Al come out of the stage door at the evening's end. Paranoid of strangers he might have been, but he took on greeting all the people who would crush against the barricades: taking pictures, signing autographs, telling him how they loved his movies: *Serpico, The Godfather, Scent of a Woman.*

He was jovial in manner, and the crowd ate it up. Watching this several times, I noted that his pattern was exactly the same. In fact, at the same point every night, he would take a pen that he had been given to sign with and would toss it high in the air to someone in the waiting crowd, to everyone's delight.

I realized then he was greeting the multitude as an acting exercise, as if playing the same scene over and over again.

Then, he would get in his waiting car, a large Escalade, and be driven around the corner where Al and the driver would trade places, with Al taking the wheel and driving himself to his house on the Hudson River or his apartment downtown.

Once when I was walking into the theatre, I met Al coming off the stage. He asked me, "Is anyone in the house?"

I thought it a strange question. "I'm just getting in. Is something wrong? Did someone say something?"

"No, I just wondered."

A brilliant actor? Yes. But a little odd, too. But genius is genius, especially if you're selling out the house every night. The reading (or whatever you want to call it) did just that. Sold every ticket in sight for all fifty-nine performances. Running into Phil Smith at the end of the run, he said to me, "Now that's a real star."

***

Al was a character, yes. A brilliant actor, but also a character. Broadway draws them like moths to its glowing lights. Here are just a few I came to know, and even love.

Gerson Werner came to work for the Shuberts in 1917 as an office boy. His uncle, Jacob Klein, was the attorney of the brothers. He built the company into what it was to become as much as anyone else with his brilliant dealings in real estate, which built their empire.

Gerson was perhaps five foot five in his raised platform shoes. He wore the wide, incredibly loud ties favored by men in the '70s. His suits were the best polyester.

Gerson had become the manager of the Imperial Theatre, and like Archie Thompson, was included in the Shubert will, and therefore could not be fired without great cause.

He often gave the bosses great cause, as when he was found carrying a .22 caliber pistol around the theatre. Nightly he rode the D train through a rough Harlem at 11:00 PM, a little Jewish man, to his apartment in Washington Heights.

He was not going to be messed with without a fight. Phil Smith found out about the gun and said no more carrying it around the theatre. If it went off and got a patron in the foot, Shubert would be on the hook for millions.

Once Gerson was approached by a woman easily in her eighties. He was her age or more. She asked, "Can I see you in your office?"

"Why?" said Gerson.

"I want to French you," the lady said.

To which Gerson curtly replied, "Madam, you are on the wrong side of Eighth Avenue."

I was assigned to do his paperwork as an apprentice, as I had for Archie Thompson. During the take-in for what would become the mega-hit *Dreamgirls,* I would spend hours with him in his small office outside of what we called the Count-Up room. There the torn ticket stubs of the night before were checked out to make sure no funny business was going on.

The many stories he told me from an earlier day tended to be racy. And with ample reason, because Mr. Lee, as Gerson called him, had made him the man who called "the madam." Why? So that one of her girls would be there to be "interviewed" by Mr. Lee, first thing in the morning. One of these girls was asked by Gerson if Mr. Lee ever got her into one of the shows in his theatres. "No," this young beauty replied.

"Well, I can do that for you. Wouldn't you like to see a show or two, maybe with your mother?"

A short time later, the same girl, after their morning "interview," thanked Mr. Shubert for passing her into a show for free. Gerson was called into Lee Shubert's office along with his uncle, Mr. Klein.

"You're fired, Gerson, for going after my girl!" said Mr. Lee. Klein then told Gerson to go outside, empty his desk, and wait. At the end of the day, Klein brought Gerson back into Mr. Lee's office, where he apologized.

"Never do that again!" screamed Mr. Lee. Gerson was sent home, still in possession of his job. He told me that happened about six times. Fired in the morning, rehired at night, for different reasons other than doing a favor for one of the madam's girls.

Once he told me he and his uncle, along with Mr. Lee, were walking along the boardwalk in Miami Beach on vacation. A girl passed and waved at Gerson, who knew him from New York.

Soon after, another girl greeted Gerson. A third girl came up as they continued to walk the boardwalk and gave Gerson a kiss, to which Mr. Lee said, "You know her, too?"

"Yes. That's Claire."

"Well, you should run for the Mayor of Miami," said Mr. Shubert.

Why Gerson shared these, the bluest of stories, with me, was anyone's guess.

Everyone knew the Shubert brothers. They owned most of the legitimate theatre houses in the country, creating a monopoly. In the mid-fifties, they were broken up by an anti-trust injunction brought against them by the government. They were not only two of the most powerful men in the theatre but also the country. There were legitimate children, like John Shubert, J.J.'s son, beloved by all, who died young in 1962. There were also illegitimate children who would work for Shubert for decades, "for obvious reasons," as Phil Smith was known to have said.

Harry Frazee built the Longacre Theatre in 1914. The prominent feature of the theatre was a ring of empty Greek helmets around the top of the ceiling. Harry was a high-living, free-wheeling entrepreneur of the day. Soon after, he bought the Boston Red Sox and turned one of the great teams in baseball into a bottom dweller by the late twenties. Of course, it started with selling Babe Ruth to the Yankees so he could produce *No, No, Nanette*. After the crash in '29, when margins were called on stocks that had been bought for ten cents on the dollar, great impresarios like Frazee were selling their theatres for nothing. The Shuberts, being ever frugal in a cash business, were happy to build their empire on the backs of men like Harry Frazee.

Gerson also benefited from the advice of his uncle, Jacob Klein, Shubert's real estate genius, and was rumored to own the land at the corner of 46th Street and Broadway. A Howard Johnson's was built on that land, and Gerson often could be seen eating there between shows.

He also allegedly owned the half block on Sixth Avenue where eventually the Crown Plaza was built. But everyone knew he was incredibly frugal. Cheap, even. A tight-wad. If your show was not selling out, he knew it and would call asking for comps for any number of doctors, relatives, friends, and even police officers who got him his pistol permit.

Robert Preston, of *The Music Man* fame, was playing around the corner at the Broadhurst in *Sly Fox*. Gerson found out that Preston drove home every night over the George Washington Bridge right past the Washington Heights apartment Gerson lived in with his wife. Gerson asked Preston, if he gave him a couple of bucks for gas, could he ride up to the Heights with him and hop out before he crossed the Bridge and went home.

Preston said yes, and everything went along fine until Preston got in a five-miles-an-hour fender bender. Gerson promptly sued Preston for severe bodily injury. Preston went up to Bernie Jacobs' office and said, "If that SOB doesn't drop his lawsuit, I will never act in any of your theatres again."

Jacobs called Gerson up to the office and reasoned, "Are you really hurt, Gerson? He was doing you a favor." Gerson dropped the lawsuit.

I remember running his paperwork up to him at the end of the intermission of my show. It was during the run of *They're Playing Our Song*, a Neil Simon show, with Lucie Arnaz in the lead. I opened the door and saw Lucille Ball sitting there, obviously getting away from the audience's attention at intermission as she was seeing her daughter's show.

Gerson politely introduced me. It was obvious to me they were old friends, and I, like everyone else, told her how much I loved her work. I rushed out the door and said, "Nice to meet you, Mrs. Arnaz." She politely said, "Thank you." Then, as I hit the front doors of the Imperial, I said to myself, "You idiot. She hasn't been Mrs. Arnaz in twenty years."

Gerson knew them all. Future stars. Chorus girls. When he finally retired, shortly before his passing, he had worked for Shubert from when he was a 17-year-old office boy in 1917 to 1993. Seventy-six years. All the while riding the A train up to his Washington Heights apartment night after night.

"What else would I do?" he once said to me.

***

Among Broadway characters, there are no better, nor crazier, than certain ushers. I'm not talking about the ushers who are the granddaughters and grandsons of a long line of ushers who have worked the theatres from their homes in what was once known as Hell's Kitchen. They are the best in a generational occupation. Taught mother to son and daughter how to do the job correctly.

It is the others, the oddballs, who do the job for $350 a week in one of the most expensive cities in the world because that's the only real job they can find. Two women—Mary Levins, an old Irish West Side woman and after her, Mary Knorr—did the hiring. Unfortunately, I was more often than not the one left to do the pleading for them to be fired. I never had the power to hire or fire the misfits under my watch. That had to be done by Mary, or Peter in the central office.

These two women were kind to the misfits, the unfortunate, the downright losers, who came to their office in the Sardi building looking for a job. Both women would say, "Well, you get to see the shows for free." That was true. And both would send the misfits to the Barrymore.

"Why me?" I would pleadingly ask.

"You tolerate them. Most managers won't take them at all."

"Alright, but if this one's half as crazy as the last—!"

"Don't worry, they promise to be good from now on."

Aileen was a Black girl from Cleveland. It's apparently colder than New York there because even in mid-summer she would dress in three layers of clothes. Her dream was to be a playwright and, to her credit, she did at least go to classes for it.

Now no one comes to New York with the plan of living in a small, rent-controlled studio for thirty years... and then going crazy. It just happens. She was in her late fifties. Eccentric? Yes, especially in her heavy sweaters. But I would not call her nuts, per se.

That was to come later. I discovered she began wearing a tin foil helmet under grandiose wigs because she claimed people were trying to get in her brain with their cell phones. I also often saw her talking to herself in a corner at the back of the theatre. A patron once asked me, "Who is that usher talking to?"

"Oh, lots of people," I replied.

I reported Aileen's behavior to Human Resources a dozen times, but they would not touch her. She needed help but never sought it because people were trying to get into her mind with their cell phones. "Weren't they?" Aileen said when I asked her.

Another was Anthony, who wore his hair in the Marcel style—black and straight—with earrings, neck jewelry, tight jeans, and the dirtiest white shirts you'd ever seen. That didn't bother me as much as the constant complaints from customers I received.

"That woman is very rude," they would say, mistaking his gender.

Antoine, as he sometimes preferred to be called, said everyone was always picking on him, cheating him out of the good shifts, blah, blah, blah. He would throw open the door of my office and go into a five-minute tirade without warning. He would call Mary Knorr twenty times a day to complain about anything and everything. It came to the point where, as responsive as she was to everyone, Mary would not answer when she saw his number on the caller ID.

The thing that drove me most crazy about Anthony was after the show he would go out to the stage door alleyway to find any actor who would talk to him, like Christian Slater.

He would then advise such a big star on how to make his performance better. Christian, amazingly, would listen to him. I told Anthony, "You are not to do that again. It's a big *no-no* in the theatre world. That's the director's job." But he persisted.

There were old eccentrics, too. George Nestor was an actor who had achieved some success in his earlier days. He looked like Adolphe Menjou, with a slight mustache and dyed hair that made him look fifteen years younger. He claimed to know everything about every theatre production ever, but those days were long past as George now approached eighty.

He was an incredible lothario with the young female staff members and, to make matters worse, young audience members, too. When I cautioned him not to behave that way at work, he said to me in his regal voice: "My job isn't to be just an usher. My job is to get laid."

One night, he came on to two young ladies who were friends of Mary Knorr. They reported his unwanted advances, and he got in trouble with her.

But George would just shrug off any dressing down. He had terrible breath because he drank during the show, and after it. (Ushers get breaks during the show when they can go off their posts.) One night after Act One, while still on duty, I saw George head straight across the street to the Rum House bar.

"Now, George, you know there's no drinking on duty."

"Do you know I'm drinking? Maybe I'm having a ."

"Just an honest guess," I said.

After that, he started heading down to the Mean Fiddler Bar near 8th avenue. I remember him dozing off asleep on the chair at his post, or completely falling down a flight of stairs in the middle of the show. He was perfectly fine afterward, being loose and loaded. I would write him up, then he might be suspended for three days. Upon returning to work, he would be a model citizen for a week. Then, on his break, I would see him head down the block and slip into the Mean Fiddler.

Many sub-ushers fell into this category of misfits. The most unforgettable was Malcolm Klotz, a smart 40-year-old who would question me about everything.

"How long have you been with the company? How many kids do you have? Where do you live? Can I come and sit in your office on my break? How much do managers make?"

All these questions would come in an onslaught. When he would walk into theatre as a substitute, the head usher, who assigns posts, without hesitation would scream, "Malcolm, up to the balcony!"

This happened so often, it became his name: *Malcolm of the Balcony*. One day, he was cleaning himself up in a subway bathroom. Don't ask me why. But he went into a toilet stall and threw his pants over the door. Someone ripped his pants off of the door—with his wallet still in them!—and ran out. Malcolm walked into the theatre in his white underwear. Another usher lent him a pair of pants six sizes too big. He worked with the playbills in one hand, while the other hand held up the borrowed pants to help prevent another embarrassment in front of the audience.

He disappeared from working in the theatres shortly afterward. What happened?

One didn't ask. George, Anthony, Eileen, Malcolm of the Balcony... what they did, they did for their own reasons.

The Wall at Joe Allen's

THE BAR AT JOE Allen's is a legendary place. One thing that makes it so special is that on the wall, not one poster of a hit show hangs. No, the walls are reserved for something else.

Bombs, turkeys, duds, dogs, and eggs (as in to lay) are among the many names for flops on the Great White Way. Only monumental duds have the dubious honor of having their posters hung on the walls of the bar on 46th Street. Only the biggest turkeys are awarded this honor and I've worked on a few.

No one intends to do a bad play on Broadway, but sometimes it just happens that way. *The Oldest Confederate Widow Tells All* sold four million copies as a book, but what happened at the Longacre Theatre, even with the wonderful Oscar winner Ellen Burstyn, was this: it played only one regular performance because the reviews were dreadful. "The oldest Confederate widow tells all, but only once," Joe Wallace, the head treasurer, would say. As a book, it was a bestseller. As a play, it was a dud.

Whose fault was it? No one really can tell. You have a major property from a successful book, a Broadway theatre, a major star of stage and screen, and nothing worked. It was a TURKEY! A

floperoonie! An outright bomb, and therefore worthy of enshrine-
ment on the wall of Joe Allen's. You walk around after one of
those in a daze as if you had been taxi-smacked in the middle of
47th Street. The truth is one becomes proud of having the window
card of that show up on the wall at Joe's, the way one is proud of
surviving a train wreck, or a tenement collapse. You've seen hard
times? Well, you should have been on that bomb.

And I had several, so let's get them out of the way before they
stink up the whole joint.

The Secret Rapture, according to the playwright David Hare,
was about the depressing nature of living under Margaret Thatch-
er. A family of civil employees is miserable, with their father's
death, his crazy widow (who was not their mother), and the general
state of postwar Britain. The "rapture" refers to the moment a
nun dies and meets her Lord. What nun? Where was the nun?
Hare, who had a big success with *Plenty* a few years before, got
into a pissing contest with Frank Rich, the critic of The New York
Times.

Rich had said *Rapture* was "a poor imitation of life." Ouch!
Hare wrote the editors that Rich "was too powerful," and a fart,
or something like that.

Dick Hummler, a good friend and Variety's critic, posted the
headline, "HARE AIRS RICH BITCH," in the best style of his
legendary paper.

David and Frank Rich argued in the papers for two weeks before
our show closed. It never does any good to fight with critics. They
file their reviews and that's it.

Truth is sometimes plays from England do not cross the water so well. That also works for some of our musicals going over there.

On opening night, my wife saw Bernard Jacobs, the president of Shubert and *The Secret Rapture* producer. She, not having the respect for, much less the downright fear of, Mr. Jacobs that those of us who worked for him did, approached him and directly asked, "Mr. Jacobs, do you like this play?"

"Oh, no, this play was a deal," Bernie said.

"A deal?" my wife asked.

"Yes, we asked Joe Papp to move *A Chorus Line* from the Shubert Theatre to another one of our houses. We wanted to put Sting in *The Threepenny Opera* in the Shubert. To make it attractive to Joe, we would produce this play in one of our theatres. But the deal for Sting in that show fell through. But Joe said, you're still going to produce *Rapture*, aren't you?" Jacobs shrugged. "No, I don't like this show."

Who's fault was it? The director? The cast? The playwright? All of the above? No one can tell.

Imaginary Friends was a show written by Nora Ephron. Marvin Hamlisch was composing the music. The show was to include musical numbers and vignettes.

It was about the rivalry between Lillian Hellman, the playwright, and the writer Mary McCarthy. Swoosie Kurtz played Hellman, and Cherry Jones was Mary McCarthy.

Nora's background was as a novelist, as in *Heartburn*, and as a screenwriter of *When Harry Met Sally*. She had enormous success in all those fields. It was perplexing to her that the audiences were not taking to her play. First, it was very literary, the field Nora was from. These two divas of words and paragraphs were not that interesting in the world of theatre, even when McCarthy said about Hellman, "Every word she writes is a lie, even *and* and *the.*"

Nora looked at us theatre people not knowing what we did or who we were. Most certainly, she was above speaking to us. When the reviews came out, they were not good.

Nina Lannen, the show's general manager, said to me, "This show is neither fish nor fowl." Meaning not really a play, not really a musical. Somewhere in between.

It closed in 76 performances. Musicals take a little longer to sink to the bottom of the sea because of their sheer mass, like aircraft carriers.

Both Nina and I were delighted, several years later, when Nora's play *Lucky Guy* had a hit run at the Broadhurst with Tom Hanks playing the newspaper columnist Mike McClary.

"Nora finally has her hit," I said to Nina Lannen when I saw her, even though we both knew the bittersweet truth that Nora Ephron had passed in 2012, the year before.

Elling was first done in London, a Simon Bent adaption. Its source was from Norwegian stories and movies about this huge simpleton and his roommate.

What can I say? It must have been better in the original language because it sure didn't work in English.

It starred Brendan Fraser, famous for *The Mummy* movies, *Gods and Monsters*, and many others. *Elling* was his first Broadway Show. Denis O'Hare was his roommate, and Jennifer Coolidge, from television and Christopher Guest's movie parodies, was the other lead. We opened mid-week, to disastrous reviews, and then it was announced we would close that Sunday.

Brendan walked around the theatre in a daze. Was this what Broadway was like? The people on the Titanic had a better chance.

I spoke to Brendan the Saturday before we closed. I said, "I'm sorry this happened this way. Please come back again. Please don't give up on Broadway."

"Thank you for talking to me. No one else has, not the producers, not the other managers, no one has said a word to me since opening night. I've felt so alone. Like it's all my fault."

Brendan has continued to work in movies and television, and was awarded the Oscar for his performance in *The Whale*, as all his other cast members have. But he has never been back to Broadway. Who could blame him, after the plane crash *Elling* was?

Sitting in Joe's later having lunch looking up at the *Elling* poster next to other Broadway disasters like *Moose Murders*, *Mati Hari*, and *Bring Back Birdie*, made me proud in a funny, weird way. I had a story to tell, because in the theatre we love the adventure of it all, even our failures.

"Boy, *Elling*, what a stinker!" I said to my lunch partner as we sat amid the noon chatter of Joe Allen's dining room.

Actors

IT WAS A CLOSE Encounter With the Star Kind. One day, going down the street on the way back to the theatre between matinee and evening performances, I ran into our star Richard Dreyfuss. We were doing a revival of Larry Gelbart's comedy *Sly Fox*, with a cast that featured Dreyfuss, Eric Stoltz, René Auberjonois, Elizabeth Berkley, and, my favorite, Professor Irwin Corey. It played the Barrymore in April 2004.

It was a hot summer's day, and he was wearing a tank-top undershirt. Someone on 47th Street driving along rolled down their window as they passed us and shouted out, "I loved you in *Jaws*!" To which Dreyfuss replied: "That was my father!"

Professor Irwin Corey, another cast member, was very proud of the fact that he would get five laughs every night for his five lines. He was in his mid-nineties when we were doing the show. He became famous doing *The Johnny Carson Show* as the world's foremost expert on everything.

An avowed left winger, he hated Ronald with a passion. He would say, "Reagan fired a whole union," meaning the air traffic controllers. That summer he played in the Broadway Show

League's Old Timers' game and got a single and ran fast to first base at ninety-five! He would live for another seven years. After *Sly Fox* was over, he would call me up and ask if my current show was selling out. He then would ask if he could see it with his son. If we weren't selling out, I would try to accommodate him. Why? Because he was Professor Irwin Corey, and he got five laughs for his five lines.

***

They are not children, as they are derided by some. They are serious adults who struggle to do their craft, or sullen art, in a hard world. I have known so many and have great respect for their struggle, their dedication, and their love of the theatre.

There are as many talented actors in New York as there are lights on Broadway. Some break through to become stars, but really, they all want something very basic: to work, to be onstage.

René Auberjonios was the lead in 1969 in *The Milliken Show*, the industrial my father wrote that year, doing his flamboyant Tony-winning character from the Broadway show *Coco* with Katherine Hepburn.

He had worked constantly over the years since and was playing Jethro Crouch in our revival. It was a small but good part. It was early in the last week of the run, a hot August day just before 7pm.

René had been riding his bike to the theatre from his West Side apartment when he turned onto 47th Street and was cut off by a cab, which caused him to fall hard on his right wrist.

In pain, René walked the bike with his left arm down to the theatre, a half block away. I was beckoned to the scene and immediately called an ambulance when I saw the pain etched on his face as he clutched his wrist.

The traffic around Times Square was always terrible, and I remembered many a time calling an ambulance and waiting eons as it turned onto our street and ever so slowly—even with those lights blaring—inched its way toward the Barrymore.

Five minutes went by this night, then almost ten. There wasn't even the sound of an ambulance approaching us. "My car is right in the parking lot next to the theatre. In fact, there it is. Let me run you over to St Luke's emergency room," I said. René and I, along with the company manager, drove over to the hospital.

On the way over René went into a lament, the actor's lament: "After this show, I don't know when I'll ever work again. I don't know if I ever will."

I dropped both of them off, and drove like a madman, returning to the Barrymore just in time for us to open the doors at 7:30pm.

Unfortunately, René had fractured his wrist and never did the show again. But his fears were short-lived about never working again. Soon after, he got the part of the firm's lead attorney in the television series *Boston Legal*, with James Spader and William Shatner. It ran for six years.

In his career, he would have over two hundred name parts, big and small. The last thing I saw him in was a low-budget movie called *First Cow*. It was about two men in the gold rush days who stole the milk of a prize animal so they could make a living selling cakes and pies to the men of an 1820s western mining camp. René had a walk-on part in the film, appearing in three scenes. He had no lines. He was listed in the credits as "Man with Raven."

No one who knew would ask why. He was working, of course. Doing a movie.

Patti LuPone

SEEING *EVITA* AT THE Broadway Theatre for the first time when Patti LuPone sang "Don't Cry for Me Argentina," you realized you were witnessing that moment when a wonderful show meets the perfect performer. You just know that this would be talked about for years as proof of how good Broadway can be on its best days.

But time moves on. Actors leave the show. The show itself ends its run, after tours, revivals, etc. Then actors must look for other work. Sometimes they find other great vehicles to appear in, sometimes they don't.

An Evening with Patti and Mandy was a review starring Patti and Mandy Patinkin, her co-star from *Evita*. In the presentation they sang previous hit songs from shows like *Sunday in the Park with George, Anything Goes*, and, of course, *Evita*. They played vignettes and sang their famous songs from "Buenos Aires" to "I Made a Hat."

Their *An Evening with Patti and Mandy* had toured the world sporadically for several years before landing at the Barrymore. It received favorable reviews and settled in for a comfortable run, if not a spectacular one.

I told Patti one night, "I could listen to you sing "A Quiet Thing" from *Flora, the Red Menace* every day of my life. I just love that song."

One day, Miss LuPone was coming to work in her car, driven by her young driver. They stopped right next to the theatre, perhaps five feet in the alleyway of the huge Morgan Stanley building next to the Barrymore.

Now, this alleyway had been closed since 9/11 and was only used for the limousines of the high-powered types of the giant brokerage. Somehow their lawyers convinced the city it was a danger to let pedestrians in this alley, unlike all the other pass-throughs in the theatre district, which remained open. They hired minimum-wage men to make sure no one blocked "their alley" at any time.

One of those men came out and knocked on the window of Patti's car as it was stopped perhaps three or four feet in their alleyway.

"We'll just be a minute. I'm the star of the show. See my picture up on the marquee. I'm Patti LuPone."

Patti then threw the door of the car open and it hit the guy. He then pushed the door closed. Patti got out of the car and slapped him on the head. With that, an international incident was declared.

As soon as I arrived at work shortly after this scene, I was called back to Patti's dressing room, where I found her in tears. She kept saying over and over: "I just wanted to go to work! Why won't they let me just go to work?" She then added, "I just tapped him."

Still in tears, she proceeded to demonstrate with a hard tap on the top of my head.

I told her I would call our security right away. It became a big showdown between Morgan Stanley's security team and Shubert. They said they had camera footage of Patti striking the man. We said he pushed her first. It wasn't all settled until Bob Wankel, now the president of Shubert, went up and spoke to the head of Morgan Stanley. Rumor had it that perhaps he said: "Do you know how much money Shubert has with you?"

At any rate, peace was restored and until this day, many years after 9/11, the alley for which they receive tax breaks still remains closed to the general public.

The fact that Miss LuPone might have a temper is widely known. You never mess with someone of Sicilian descent. According to Jean Claude, the owner of the acclaimed restaurant Pierre Au Tunnel, which was across from the Barrymore: "The only person ever asked to vacate the premise in fifty years was Patti LuPone."

One night, she came in very late after the bartender Allen had closed his bank and locked up for the night. She demanded a drink from the eighty-year bartender, a gentleman's gentleman.

In his youth, Allen played the clarinet in the Dorsey Brothers Band. After harsh words between them, she became the only eviction Jean Claude could ever remember.

One night she was with friends, one of whom was my friend Joe Traina, having a few drinks at Gallagher's Steak House on 52nd Street. When they were on their way out, Patti noticed something was going on at The Roseland Ballroom across the street. The place that hosted musical acts from Beyonce to The Beach Boys. Sadly, it closed in 2014 with Lady Gaga doing the final show.

Patti wanted to go over and see what was happening. It was now well after when the Roseland Ballroom show had begun. The doors were locked from the outside and no one was in the lobby area on the other side.

Then Patti noticed there was still a light coming from behind the box office curtains, which had been lowered. Patti went over to the window and hollered: "Patti LuPone! Patti LuPone! *Evita*! *Evita*! Patti LuPone! *Anything Goes*! *Evita*! Patti LuPone!"

After twenty seconds, they heard a voice from behind the drawn curtain, saying: "No habla ingles." It was Salsa Night at Roseland.

The show proceeded without incident after that "little" slap, but business began to slump before the scheduled end of the run. Both Patti and Mandy were consummate professionals when it came to performing the show and how they treated the crew backstage, but the public started to lose interest.

Patti would often ask me how business was when I would run into her backstage. I told her honestly that business was slowing, to which she said in great diva style: "Yes, Mandy and I are stars, but we're fading stars."

Nothing could be further from the truth. Since we did that show, both of them have been continuously working.

Philip Seymour Hoffman

AT THE AGE OF forty-four, he was considered one of America's greatest living actors. His film work had garnered high praise for over a decade, including an Academy Award-winning performance as Truman Capote.

It was through a montage of character roles that he had risen to prominence, but that was not all. He had also found time to star onstage in O'Neill, and to direct plays at his theatre company, the Labyrinth.

He was to play Willie Loman at that young age in a revival of Arthur Miller's *Death of a Salesman*, which was to be directed by my old friend and adversary, Mike Nichols.

Through the years, whenever Mike and I would run into each other, he would mercilessly tease me about "how important" I acted when we both knew that I was not. Mike was a card and had that great cutting wit.

I once got slightly even with him. When taking Mary Louise Parker and Mike backstage once, all I did was talk to her, telling her how wonderful she was in the series *Weeds*. I ignored Mike completely until I got a jibe in when I said: "Oh, Mike, *The Graduate* was such a wonderful movie. You had such potential."

Anyhow, it was a game we played for years, and I was delighted when it became clear that after all the time since Whoopi Goldberg's one-woman show we had become like old theatre warriors: the fear I once had of him had transformed into a respect and appreciation of his great talent.

Nichols had a guaranteed hit on his hands with Hoffman in a Miller play. I had run into Arthur Miller a few years before, as we were both crossing Times Square. He was tall and distinguished. I introduced myself and said, "I'm sorry your play *The Ride Down Mount Morgan* closed."

"Well, the problem is advertising is so expensive. That's because the Jewish guys who run your company"—(he was Jewish himself)—"don't get along with the Jewish guys who run the New York Times."

It was true: the Shuberts and Sulzbergers did not get along. They had been adversarial since an expose about Jacobs and Schoenfeld had run years before, which they felt was unfair. It was about how they had taken over the company, and how they were overpaid. It was judged in litigation those were both false accusations.

I would have loved to have heard Miller's take on Hoffman's interpretation of the role, if not the strange loner himself. Distant is the word I would use to describe the late Philip Seymour Hoffman. He didn't return greetings to anyone. Not me, not the other cast members, not the crew or dressers.

PHILIP SEYMOUR HOFFMAN   199

On the upside, the show itself was a huge success. Philip, despite his young age, was wonderful in the role and deserved his Tony nomination.

Bill Camp, who played Charlie, Willie Loman's best friend in the show, loved to play softball in Central Park. He was once approached by two young filmmakers, also players in the League, who asked Bill if he could get them an interview with Philip to see if he would do a five-line part in their short movie.

"I don't know how I could do that? He only speaks to me onstage," Bill told them.

Also, from early on, it became harder and harder to bring stars backstage to see Hoffman. He had "left the theatre" I was told by the stage managers a minute after the curtain when I had Annette Benning standing next to me.

Two weeks later, her husband, Beatty, came by the theatre and asked to see Philip. I had seen our star on occasion filing out the west alley of the theatre with the audience, coat collar pulled up, acting as if he were simply another patron. So, I tried to be clever. I took Warren to the west alley and there saw my stagehand Victor with his nose poking out of the pass door.

He saw Warren and then made a pointing gesture as if to say, "He's here." Warren and I went through the door and found Philip pulling up his pants.

"Oh, Warren, not many people catch me here," Hoffman said.

The next day I was told in no uncertain terms by the Company Manager, "That is not to happen again."

Everyone had to go through the stage door—period. It was funny then when Warren Beatty came by the theatre the next day with an older lady whom I assumed was an investor. After the show, I was actually on my hands and knees looking for a patron's earring when I heard my ticket taker John Barbaretti, whom I always called "my assistant manager," yelling out to Beatty: "Everyone has to go through the stage door."

Warren and his investor headed out the wrong alleyway to find Philip where we had the previous day. Warren shouted back: "I know where he is."

I never heard about it. He obviously missed Hoffman.

Afterward, most of the cast would hang out at the Glass House Tavern across the street. There was a table reserved for the Loman family: namely Philip, his two sons Finn Wittrock and Andrew Garfield, and his wife in the show, Linda Edmond.

But once in a while on the way to pick up my car between 8th and 9th Avenues on 47th Street, I would see Hoffman walking back toward the theatre from 9th Avenue and I would swear he had a beer or two in him. It struck me as odd because I had heard through the grapevine that he was supposed to be off the sauce because he was a recovering drug addict.

It was only at those times when he would say a quick, "Hello." Or, "We have to stop meeting like this."

Hoffman's mother Marilyn, a sweet little old lady, came by the last week of the show to see her son's performance. She reminded me of my grandmother, whom I adored. I briefly spoke to Hoffman about meeting her at the theatre, and he gave me a shrug of indifference.

Within two years, Hoffman was found dead of a heroin overdose in the bathroom of his rented apartment around the corner from where his girlfriend and their three children lived. His girlfriend had made him live away from the children because of his drug use.

Phil had just finished filming scenes in the final two chapters of the *Mockingjay* movie franchise for $20 million. Whatever demons that were there—and I had seen them—had driven him into the arms of the dragon he had fought off for so long, since he was in rehab at 23.

As sad in the end as Willie Loman himself: Arthur Miller's broken and lonely salesman.

The New Century

ABOUT SIX MONTHS AFTER the 9/11 tragedy, I stood saying a prayer late one night after the show.

It was eerily still. I noticed a police car had pulled up behind my car. After my prayer, I got in my car and slowly drove away. It was then I noticed that I had driven the wrong way down a one-way street. But the cop did not follow me: there was a reverence for what had happened, and he understood.

Our great city came roaring back after 9/11. It burst into a flood of tourism that chased the porn shops of a bygone era away. The new policing policies had gotten officers out of the patrol cars in the '90s and returned them to standing on posts on the corners of Times Square.

This had turned the streets into a safer and more civilized place. Crimes like panhandling, which in the old days often led to outright robbery, were now enforced and stopped by the cop on the beat.

What came was a new theatre district of Disney and renovated hotels, theme park-like businesses like the Toys 'R' US store where a full-size T. Rex dinosaur lurked amid the dolls and bikes, rearing its head up to roar every fifteen minutes. It was like something straight out of the Tom Hanks movie *Big*. There was a newfound joyous innocence beginning to flourish. The old Times Square was fading behind the glitter of the new Hersey Chocolate store, Forrest Gump Shrimp, and even more chocolate in the shape of the M&Ms store.

We on Broadway played our part in the resurrection of the Big Apple's spirit with some of the best productions in living memory. At both high summer and Christmas, the streets were so crowded that you had to be careful on corners, with people heading in two directions.

The Barrymore remained a prized house where shows with major stars played. We had *Exit the King* starring Geoffrey Rush in a Tony-winning performance. The stellar cast also included Susan Sarandon, William Sadler, Lauren Ambrose, and Andrea Martin.

After the performance, Geoffrey Rush would relax in the same place in the stagedoor alleyway, with a Heineken beer in each hand, or with a Heineken in one hand and a cigarette in the other. He stood directly under the exit sign where he would take pictures with friends, and friends of friends, who came backstage.

He was making his Broadway debut, and though he worked incredibly hard onstage, I think I can safely say he loved every minute. He would go to Joe Allen's after the show, living it up as the Broadway star he was.

Susan Sarandon would bring a small poodle to the theatre almost every night. After she entered the stage door, in the safety of the alleyway, she would put the puppy down and he would run up the one flight of stairs to her dressing room, knowing the way. I saw this several times until one night he got right next to me and stopped dead in his tracks, looking up at me. It was as if he knew I was the guy who could say: "Oh, no, no dogs in the theatre." As if I would ever do that to anyone, never mind a star of Susan Sarandon's magnitude. I definitively said to the dog, "Go!" He then scampered up the steps to Susan's room.

I ran into Susan several years later as she was waiting in line to enter the theatre, seeing a different show. She said, "They're doing a musical of *Bull Durham*. Can you imagine that?"

It was an adaptation of her very successful movie with Kevin Costner and Tim Robbins, who was to become her partner for many years. "Yes, how are they going to do the baseball onstage?" I said.

Then the ego of a fabulous actress entered as she said: "And who are they going to get to play me?"

But not all such spinoffs on Broadway are "sure things." For example, *Ring of Fire* was a review of Johnny Cash songs. He had passed three years before, but two of his children were around and involved in Richard Maltby Jr.'s production.

What can one say as to why some "jukebox" musicals work, and others don't? *Ring of Fire* failed because, well, who knows? The majority of reviews were poor, even though Cash's music remains as popular as ever.

***

Every spring, Equity Fights Aids would do a special fundraising presentation called *The Easter Bonnet Show*. The dressers and costume people would make the most outrageous hats, usually with the theme of their show. Two characters from *Urinetown*—the big cop, Jeff McCarthy, and the Little Sally character, played by Spencer Kayden—would come out and joke about the performances.

When the Johnny Cash presentation was over, Little Sally cracked: "How is *Ring of Fire* still running?"

"They're holding out for the Tony nominations," replied Jeff McCarthy.

The audience burst out in laughter, knowing nominations were not only highly unlikely but downright impossible. Sitting in the audience I found that sad because your show is your show and you root for it. "Words are only words..."

ACT FOUR

THE LAST ACT

What happened??

YOU'LL RECALL I MENTIONED that the Broadway Show *DA* was produced for $125,000 in 1978, while *The Front Page* with Nathan Lane and John Goodman was produced in 2015 for $4,000,000. What happened that drove costs up?

I asked three Broadway general managers who have been on the scene for most of that time. The first has produced on Broadway and Off, and has been general manager on long-running Off-Broadway international hits.

"The cost of advertising now is astronomical and has grown enormously over the years. Print in The Times, at least some of it is mandatory, and producers—by that I mean the many people who 'go in' on Broadway shows—in this day and age have to compete with corporations like Disney, or mega producers like Scott Rudin, who often takes two pages to advertise the three or four shows he has running at once. Along with that, there are websites, television advertising, and the rest.

We also live in a time when designers on Broadway want the best instruments, for the most spectacular effects. In college, I was told that you could light a show with nine instruments. In this age, hundreds and hundreds of instruments are used, and the rental of the lights, the electronic boards, and the musical synthesizers are all enormously expensive in comparison to the way it was years ago. You rent these things because it's much cheaper than buying them upfront.

When it comes to labor—meaning stagehands, musicians, and even actors—costs have gone through the roof when it comes to Broadway.

I always dreamed it would be wonderful to get labor to agree to a twenty or forty-year contract with a guaranteed raise written in for cost of living. But it hasn't worked out that way. The stagehands go by the book, the Local #1 contract, and those rules were written in the 1940s when a stagehand was making $2.00 an hour. That means overtime was $4.00. Now the house head makes $80 an hour and overtime is $160, plus pension, plus annuity, all paid for by the attraction. And those contracts are renegotiated every three or four years, all benefiting labor in new ways.

It's all paid for by raising the ticket prices, but the problem is that it makes going to the theatre a special event. So, people go once a year on their anniversary, instead of five or six times like they used to. Also, tourists—whether they are from here or across the country or overseas—are willing to pay the top prices that float the industry because everyone is rich on vacation.

Adventurous new work is not what they choose. As a result, when it comes to Broadway, producers make the safe play and go with revivals with stars, or known commodities, like new musicals from famous movies or books.

There will always be a Broadway, but I can't see the costs coming down. The days of the single producer are over. The risks are now shared by a dozen or more producers.

I remember Manny Azenberg, legendary Broadway producer, telling me a year or two ago, 'If you want people to think that you won a Tony, just run on the stage with everyone else at the Tony Awards when they announce Best Play or Best Musical. Half of the producers do not know the other half. They might even shake your hand. Then people watching will think you won a Tony Award.'"

***

The second general manager I spoke to has managed long-running musicals for most of her career. In the theatre, we call that luck.

"When you asked me the question about what has driven up the cost of Broadway over the last four decades, I immediately thought of rising labor costs, which go up 3% a year.

Then I thought of the many other factors that have driven up costs over time. Now my experience is musicals, so let me stick to that. A great addition to the cost with musicals these days is the development phase. First, you have to raise money to do the workshop here in town. There are many types of those, and in the most expensive format, you can spend close to a million dollars on the workshop alone. You do these workshops to involve other partners or producers. Because, usually, you want to go out of town, to a regional theatre where, with the money you give them, they will produce your show. Places like La Jolla, Paper Mill, Fifth Avenue. The purpose of this is to test your show, maybe even improve it, before it comes to New York to go in front of the critics, and—more importantly these days—the public. Because more and more it is word of mouth that sells shows, and The New York Times cannot shut a show right away like it could twenty y ears ago.

The reason now is because if you come into town, you better come in with a huge contingency fund to help you get through the early months.

It all adds up to millions because advertising is now as important as ever and there are fifty ways to spend that money on television, radio, newspapers—not only The Times, but that newspaper is still important. If it does come to New York, you pay for another load-in. Sometimes new scenery, costumes. All very expensive.

However, Broadway has had many things going for it over the last decade or so. Broadway became cool again to young people because of new and inventive shows like Rent, *the brilliant production of* The Lion King, *television shows like* Glee. *All made Broadway hip again and spurred incredible business before this terrible virus came along, which shut us all down.*

Dynamic pricing has helped too, whereby you can sell tickets at different amounts according to demand. In the mid-1980s, when I came to this business, people would ask me why I wanted to work in a dying business. Well, it didn't work out that way, and the industry flourished.

In the old days, the theatre owners did all the negotiations with the unions. Now we have a Labor Committee with people like Nina Lannen, Charlotte Wilcox, and other general managers who are there to express the interest and concerns of people who actually produce the shows and pay all the bills.

I believe Broadway will come back after this time. What is Times Square without Broadway? For that matter, what is New York? You mentioned before that tourism has made producers turn to well-known product from movies, books, famous singers, etc.

But I find it heartening that the biggest successes of recent years have come from original material.

Shows like Hamilton, Fun Home, Rent, Avenue Q, Dear Evan Hanson, *and* Hadestown. *Those are the shows that have won awards and prospered. The world will come back to these streets, to Broadway, once again. I believe that."*

***

The third I questioned has been both a general manager and company manager for close to thirty-five years. Well-respected and intelligent, his reputation in the business is impeccable.

"The question is what drove the price of doing Broadway, and therefore paying to go see shows up?

One is, of course, linked to the other. The first thing that popped into my mind was that, unlike Norma Desmond, who said in Sunset Boulevard, *'The movies got small,' on Broadway the shows got big.*

After Cats, Phantom, Les Mis, *and* Lion King, *productions became spectacular, and it became what people wanted. No, even more than that, expected.*

With the grand scale, the designers became a major force in the business. With that, the directors and others on the creative teams demanded and expected the best, meaning the most expensive. Everything went up. The sets, the costumes, everything. Add to that the increasing demands of the labor—has Broadway ever won a strike?—and you have a constant upward spiral of production costs.

Throw in the many different types of advertising a show must now buy, and to a degree, you have your answer. Of course, this is covered by raising ticket prices, which the public begrudgingly accepts.

If you are going to Broadway, you expect to go for some coin for the ticket, especially for this season's hot show.

I will tell you something else. The cost of going to professional sports went through the roof and almost made going to Broadway seem reasonable. I remember once a revival of one of those major musicals was coming to a large Broadway house. There was a scene, one scene, where a bench was required. Well, the show had been touring the world with many productions. We had several benches in storage from those productions. The designer and the director wanted a slightly longer bench. We went to the producer, and he agreed that we had to build a new bench. It's not a big thing, but it just shows how everyone is afraid to say no to the creatives. That is true even more so in this day when there are no longer single producers, but dozens on a major musical.

David Merrick could say, 'No, we have a bench and it's just fine.'

Producers now would rather spend whatever the creative team wants to keep them happy."

Hit with the "Lucky Stick"

My friend Jason Kincaid, a long-time soap opera star, along with playing many other television and musical roles, before becoming a beloved professor to young actors, had an expression he loved to use. When an actor he knew suddenly got a big break, like a major movie or a television series out of the blue (and it does happen more than you can imagine), he would say, "They got hit with the Lucky Stick."

Simply put, why does one actor succeed while another flounders when they are both remarkably talented?

Steve Olsen, my friend and the owner of the West Bank Cafe, where August Wilson and I used to drink, told me this story.

A former bartender of his got the understudy role in Sam Shepard's *Fool for Love* Off-Broadway. He got to go on for the last two weeks of the run before the show closed. Steve saw his performance and said to an agent he knew, Gene Parseghian, "You have to see this guy. He's great."

The agent went backstage and talked to the actor after he saw the show. He said, "I came to see you for this play I'm casting, but you're not right for it. However, there is a television series out in LA looking for a male lead and I think you're perfect for it. So, if you can get out there, I can get you an audition."

The actor bought a plane ticket, and the rest is history. His name was Bruce Willis, and the series was *Moonlighting*. He, as Jason would have said, was hit by the proverbial "Lucky Stick."

Chez Josephine was a restaurant on 42nd Street across the street from the West Bank. The owner was the son of the legendary Josephine Baker. It was one of the favorite places of Bob and Mindy Rich when they were in town from Buffalo. Their name was Rich, and they were.

Bob owned Rich Foods. His father had owned it before him, and also owned the Buffalo Bills when Marv Levy was the coach and O.J. Simpson was the running back. Chris Curtis was the resident piano player at Chez Josephine. He would play for Bob and Mindy Broadway show tunes nightly, along with songs from his new show called *Chaplin*. Mindy, in love with the theatre, talked Bob into producing it, and Chris Curtis, out of the blue, was hit by the "Lucky Stick."

Now you must know every piano player in a club in New York has a musical in their back pocket and would love to play a few songs to a producer and have it picked up for production. However, the odds of that happening are astronomical, but not for lucky Mr. Curtis, a charming man who loved to be at the Barrymore every night *Chaplin* played.

Another story I love to tell about Chez Josephine is about the priest at Holy Cross Church, Father Pete. A frequent visitor to

Chez Josephine at night, the owner actually gave him his own key to the place. As a result, in the morning at 8 o'clock, he could be seen sitting in the window having a morning libation. He would wave at police walking down the street from their precinct, on their way to their posts for the day, to come in and join him for a drink. He knew them all because when he had too much the night before at Josephine or the West Bank across the street, he had his own call over the police radio: "Five hundred feet, Father Pete." Then a squad car would come and pick him up and take him to the rectory between 8th and 9th Avenues about five hundred feet away.

But before Broadway, Mindy and Bob first produced *Chaplin* at the La Jolla Playhouse in California. All the costumes from the La Jolla production were in living color. When it came to New York, they were changed to black and white like Chaplin's movies. They were replaced with techno-color ones only at the end of the show.

Tom Meehan, my old friend from *I Remember Mama*, was hired to help punch up the book of the show. He once asked me which lines I thought he wrote. It was an easy question. "The funny ones," I said.

The show emphasized Chaplin's failed marriages, his political beliefs, and his brilliant movies like *The Great Dictator*. Tom Meehan told me a story, not depicted in the show, about when Burgess Meredith, later of *Rocky* fame, told Chaplin that he was in love with his wife, Paulette Goddard. That was after she was involved with the genius George Gershwin, before cutting him off, causing depression in him. The great composer died shortly after, at the age of thirty-nine. "Just take her," Charlie said to Meredith, suffering from a lack of faithfulness himself.

Tom Meehan told me he once spoke to Chris and asked him who his competition on Broadway was. Chris dutifully went through the list of other musicals opening during that season. "No," Tom said, "your competition is Stephen Sondheim and Leonard Bernstein. They've seen what they can do, and now it's your turn."

The show, which featured a marvelous Tony-nominated performance by Rob McClure, never quite caught on. We were gone in four months. The wonderful producers, Bob and Mindy Rich, gave it the best shot they could, but to no avail.

I remember Rob McClure's dressing room filled with little Chaplin dolls, bowler hats, canes, and other "Little Tramp" memorabilia.

Chris Curtis came into my office in the Barrymore heartbroken at our closing. He told me he had a contract to do the show in Russia, and also South America. I thought to myself, a month in St. Petersburg, and two months in Brazil, what an adventure! But sorrow was all he could feel, as his Broadway run was ending.

I would always ask a playwright or a composer, whose work came to the Barrymore, what they were working on next. The purpose of this was to get their mind for a moment off of this show. To let them know there was life after their opening night had come and gone.

It has played around the world ever since. Life does go on after Broadway, and everyone loves the "Little Tramp."

Still lucky, I've always thought, about the broken-hearted man who sat across from me in my office that January day.

Movie Stars

JAMES BOND WAS COMING to Broadway. And it was made even more exciting because Daniel Craig's wife Rachel Weisz, who won an Oscar for *The Constant Gardner*, was to appear with him in Harold Pinter's *Betrayal*. It didn't matter that it was an old play because the story's brilliant conceit was that the last scene was actually the first scene. It was told in reverse as it went through the story of a dissolving marriage. It's the type of play that is even better on second viewing, thanks to this twist.

The lines were down the block on the day the box office opened, simply because of the beautiful movie stars. I witnessed people walk up to the box office on several occasions and say, "Two for James Bond."

But more than anything, the show was being "dug out" under the new scalping laws that now governed the city. Scalping did occur in the old days, but it was controlled by professionals in the box office and the licensed brokerages. Every tourist on a week's vacation is rich, or at least acts that way, in that they are willing to pay premium prices to see the "hot" show. "Ice" is what it was called, because it cools off a hot ticket. In the old days, when it was regulated, there was a feeling that if one became too greedy, it would attract the attention of the New York Attorney General's office. There had been an investigation in the past and people had gone to jail for being involved. So, though it went on, it was somehow controlled.

It was odd that, though it was illegal in New York, it was legal right across the river in New Jersey. I knew the assistant treasurer at the Majestic who left his good-paying job on *Phantom* to open his own brokerage on the other side of the Hudson.

When the restrictive laws went out, everyone got involved, all the way down to kids in their parents' basements. They started with rock concerts, then they moved on to everything else, including Broadway.

Also, the criminal element became involved, which led to counterfeit tickets, digging out handicapped seats that sell for much less, and selling them as full-priced tickets to a naïve public.

I saw a young Spanish girl in her early twenties in line four or five times. I asked her leaving the lobby one matinee: "Big fan of Pinter?"

"Who?" she asked.

"The playwright," I said.

Then she replied: "No, I just do this for a guy I know."

Also, "bots" had just entered the scene: automatic computer programs that bought blocks of tickets en masse. They would become infamous a couple of years later when the smash hit *Hamilton* came along.

The run of *Betrayal* nearly sold out before the first preview. It was the night of that first preview when Scott Rudin, the producer, decided latecomers were not to be permitted in at all. Refunds were not to be given at the box office. Tardy patrons had to send their unused tickets to the play's production office on 44th Street.

But when you have gotten a babysitter, been joined by friends, and paid for an expensive dinner, only to arrive a minute late to the theatre to then be told you cannot see the show...? Well, it pisses people off.

Where was the warning on the ticket? Or the wall of the box office? Or anywhere? Add to that, nearly all the tickets for the entire run were now sold, meaning there were no replacement tickets for future performances to be had. Nothing, no way, no how.

"Just go home and mail in your tickets," was what disgruntled latecomers were told. They took their anger out on who they could, the person right in front of them; namely, the manager. It was all very confusing to me since the first scene change was eight minutes into the play, and that change lasted two minutes. Why couldn't they be allowed in then, right?

Again, sixteen minutes into the play, there was another scene change lasting another two minutes. My ushers could have seated an army regiment in either of those breaks, ending all the consternation, but it was forbidden.

Rudin still does not let latecomers be seated at his produced plays, but the difference is since *Betrayal* that the policy is now printed clearly on the tickets and posted on the lobby wall.

I felt like the Grinch who stole Christmas when a young woman sprinted into the lobby and, out of breath, fell to her knees as she frantically searched for her ticket. She had run from Grand Central Station. The play had just started, and she burst into tears when I told her she could not enter.

Profusely, on her knees, she begged me to enter. But I was forced to say that was not possible. There was a rare happy ending to this. She wrote Mike Nichols, and he gave her two of his house seats. But for the rest who showed up even thirty seconds late, they were out of luck.

Early on, it was all bedlam. In the first preview, two people showed up with counterfeit tickets. Rather than having them wait in the lobby, the ticket taker had them stand against the back curtains in the theatre, since the lobby was packed. Rudin saw them and said, "What are they doing in here?"

I explained it was a mistake and politely asked them to leave the theatre. Then I went on to put out the next fire for people who had bought "handicapped" seats. For them, since they were not in a wheelchair or walker, I had to take them back to the box office and explain they owed us another $200.

After we took the curtain up, I was surrounded by a group of eight people who were two minutes late. They proceeded to quiz me: "Should we sue?"

"Just send your tickets in for a refund."

"Where? How do we know you're not lying?"

"Hey, it says on this ticket you can be seated 'at the desecration of the management.' You're the manager! Show some desecration!"

They all stood around me like a mob and wrote in letters saying I told them to sue the theatre, which I had not. They were wet-cat angry, and who could blame them?

These conversations were repeated over and over during the run of the show, the next four months. I needed all this like a hole in the head.

It disgusted me to see good money being thrown down the drain, or in the trash can, as I had seen one Saturday night when a man and his date turned up late.

He said to me, "I paid a thousand dollars each for these two seats."

"I'm sorry, but there is absolutely nothing I can do."

He immediately walked over to the trashcan in the lobby, threw the two tickets in, and left with his friend.

The assistant stage manager, Kathryn McKee, and I would stand in front of the theatre and look at six minutes after eight—the curtain time—for people running on 47th toward the theatre. If we saw patrons running, we would hold the curtain.

The play was only an hour and a half long, but it was determined we had to start the show by seven minutes after.

I was contacted by the Secret Service and told that Meryl Streep and Hillary Clinton were coming to the theatre the next night. I didn't know how to break the news to them when I was told: "They might be a little late because she's attending a fundraiser."

How could I refuse entry to the then Secretary of State?? I told the company manager Penny Daulton, and the next day got a call from Scott Rudin at my home in New Jersey and he said, "They are there by ten minutes after, or you start the show and deny them entry."

Well, I thought to myself, I could screw myself in two ways: Ms. Meryl Streep could call up the heads of Shubert and complain about my "rudeness." Or Hillary might have my taxes audited. I am joking, of course. Well, half-kidding.

I was never so happy to see two ladies arrive at 8:08 with two minutes to spare. As Hillary Clinton walked by me, she held up a heavy briefcase she was carrying and gave me a fist bump. That was one vote to the good, I can assure you.

***

Our production, though poorly reviewed, grossed 17 million dollars in fourteen weeks. As I said, movie stars sell tickets.

The set for *Betrayal* was on tracks on the stage floor. One night, a screw or a bolt got stuck in the tracks. This meant the scenery could not be changed automatically. A work call by the stagehands was required to take up parts of the stage floor and fix the problem. Again, there was a meeting with the four cast members as to whether they would perform that night.

It was decided that the stagehands would bring the set pieces on before each scene, then strike them and set up the next scene. The cast agreed to play the show, but this added forty-five minutes to the running time.

The next day Daniel Craig saw me walking into the theatre and said about performing without a functioning set: "I'll never do that again."

***

I feared it was Mike Nichols' last Broadway show. Mike had become very frail by then, though still up as ever to teasing poor me. He came up to me on Opening Night with his wife Diane Sawyer, and in front of Peter Entin and Mark Schweppe, my bosses, before we opened the theatre, asked: "Dan, can you go up to your office and get me three fingers of vodka?"

He clearly wanted to soothe his nerves. But liquor in a manager's office is frowned upon.

Everybody would've been thinking, "What a big mouth Mike is landing poor Dan here in hot water." But I thought quickly on my feet, "Oh, Mike, I don't have anything like that in my office, but I'll go to the lower lobby bar and get you some."

"No, that's alright," he said, the joke played.

We ended the run of *Betrayal* in the first week of January 2014. I felt as beat up as if I had been in combat, even if it had been an enormous financial success. All these people yelling at me, saying: "I'll never come back to Broadway again!"

It all was to occur again on Larry David's *A Fish in the Dark*. The manager of the Cort Theatre had to call the executives of Shubert up and say, "I can't guarantee that violence will not occur in the lobby due to the many confrontations over this policy."

Toward the end of the run of *Betrayal*, I brought my copy of *Death of a Salesman* backstage to have Mike Nichols sign it, as he was sitting in the stage manager's office. Mike had bought us all, cast and crew, beautiful bound copies of the script of *Salesman* for opening night gifts for that show. Ever the joker, he signed my copy in his Polish name: Mikhail Peschkowsky. He and his family had fled Europe in 1939 as the Nazi terror was surrounding them.

He handed me the signed script and said, "Look! I bet you could get a lot of money for it." Then, "Some dead guy signed it."

Now that Mike has passed, I would never sell it in a thousand years.

Boom Time

IN THE DECADE AFTER 2010, Broadway entered into the boom time we could only dream of in the bad old days when I was chasing ladies of the night from underneath the Lyceum marquee.

More than ten shows began to gross over one million dollars per week. Some of those shows, like *Wicked* and *Lion King,* would gross over two million a week.

The shows being produced also reflected the famous movies they were drawn from. Subjects the visitors from Iowa would know right away, such as *Aladin, Big Fish*, and *The Addams Family*. Or what we call "jukebox musicals," like *Jersey Boys*, which was about the rise of The Four Seasons.

This jukebox hit was the brainchild of Rick Elice, a former press agent and union brother. Marshall Brickman, the writer of several of Woody Allen's early movies, was brought on board to polish up the book. Marshall said after the show became a smash hit: "It has always been my dream to lie on my deathbed surrounded by my children and their accountants and now, thanks to *Jersey Boys*, that will happen."

Then the phenomenon *Hamilton* came along, Lin-Manuel Miranda's hip-hop examination of the history of America's forefathers.

"A big hit rises the tide and floats all boats," Gerry Schoenfeld used to say. This was true of *A Chorus Line* in the 1970s, but *Hamilton* was beyond that. I had many a conversation with Lin in the Polish Tearoom or the Cafe Edison. He had gone to school with my daughter Chelsea at Wesleyan University and they had done a student film together called *Cousin Cocaine*. Lin had *In the Heights* playing, his show about Washington Heights, at the Richard Rogers Theatre on 46th Street.

After *Hamilton* opened, when I passed Lin on the street, he would be wearing headphones, dark glasses, and a hoody over his head. I would get no more than a wave as he walked quickly past. I completely understood. The world wanted tickets to his show, and he didn't have them to give.

The wildest scalping story I ever heard was about a party of friends of my cousin who bought tickets to *Hamilton* the previous October to see the July 9th performance the following year. But little did they know it would be Lin Manuel Miranda's final performance in the show. They were offered $8,000 for each ticket. Yes, that's right. $8,000 each. Crazy, but true.

The next show presented at the theatre was Lorraine Hansbury's *A Raisin in the Sun*, which had first been done at the Barrymore in 1959. Denzel Washington was to star in a modern revival of the show. I had taken him around the theatre after a matinee of *Betrayal* and remembered him staring out at the house from the stage as if he was imagining what it would be like. I had seen him do the original *A Soldier's Play* Off-Broadway, and he was a wonderful stage actor. My daughter would later have a scene in *The Equalizer* movie with him, but it was left on the cutting room floor, a familiar story for many actors starting out.

The next week I was called into Mark Schweppe's office. He was now the Theatre Operations Manager, and he told me that they would like me to go to the Jacobs, formerly the Royale where *Song and Dance* had played. He wanted me to go and work on the Irish musical *Once*. The reason being, or so I was told by Mark, that Scott Rudin had requested a Black manager to work on the *Raisin* play since he was going to have the same late seating policy and he felt it would go better if an African-American manager was there!

I could give a hoot about "the policy," as long as this move meant patrons would not be yelling at me nightly. *Once* was a marvelous, moving musical about two street musicians in Dublin based on the movie of the same name. The set was a bar, and at intermission, patrons could go onstage and order a drink. The Irish music, coupled with a moving story about this Eastern European girl and her family living in Dublin, was loved by the audience.

Rudin had become very important to Shubert and would go on to produce four shows a year for them over the next few seasons, including several blockbusters like *Hello Dolly* with Bette Midler and *To Kill a Mockingbird* with Jeff Daniels.

Rudin has always had a great sense of what the audience on Broadway—and in movies—wants.

All I have to say is once we were very friendly, chatting in the lobby before shows all the time, but now after *Betrayal,* things had changed.

I returned to the Barrymore for a magical new show from England called *The Curious Incident of the Dog in the Nighttime.* It did not feature a star of stage or screen but won the Olivier Award in London for Best Play. In the "boom time," it would go on to win five Tony Awards, including Best Actor for Alex Sharp, Best Scenic Design, and of course, Best Play.

I had at "my theatre" the best show on Broadway again. I would take friends backstage to show them the amazing intricacies of the set: steps that came out of the back wall, creating the illusion that Christopher (Alex Sharp's character) was climbing the wall by magic. The play was filled with the director Marion Elliot's brilliant stagecraft.

***

It was at this time change was in the wind for Shubert and its managers. Upon Schoenfeld's death in 2008, Robert Wankel moved into the President's chair with Phil Smith moving up to the Chairperson's role. For five or six years, everything remained the same. Then things started to happen. The way the contract read was that management could replace whoever they wanted without cause at any time. By the following spring, seven theatre managers were given notice.

Yes, two had serious drinking problems, whereby they would miss coming to the theatre for shows without excuse. But there was nothing bad you could say about the other five, who had all been a long time with the company. They wanted to replace the veteran managers with a younger group that would be specially trained by Mark Schweepe, to do the job exactly the way upper management wanted. When I was called in, I couldn't help but feel that the whole *Betrayal* experience had soured Shubert on me, so I said, "Well, I've been with the company thirty-six years. I was thinking this was going to be my last season, anyway."

What did it matter? I just wanted a last season on "the boards" for the company I had been with for so long. I wanted to go out standing on my feet, as it were, my goal being the age of sixty-five and full pension. I think I was granted that because of Peter Entin and, more likely, the Chairman of Shubert, Phil Smith. After almost four decades with Shubert, I most certainly thought I deserved the dignity of that. So we agreed that this would be my last season with the company.

I loved every one of the seventeen old Shubert theatres and had worked in them all. I had never taken a penny from anyone who wanted to see a sold-out show and never would. I took pride in what I did, as simple as it was, in the starry constellation of the Broadway theatre.

I remember Gerson Werner telling me how it was when Lee Shubert died, leaving J.J. Shubert in total control of the Company. The first thing J.J. did was to go across 44th Street and empty Lee's safe. Soon after, Lee's "people" were let go.

The top executive of Shubert automatically becomes the most powerful man in the American theatre because, simply put, Broadway theatre doesn't happen in a vacuum. It happens in a special place, at a special time. Or, how about, without a theatre you don't have a show.

I was told to "do this" and "do that" a little differently, and sent back to the Barrymore.

***

My relationship with the company manager of *Curious Incident* was never good. She brought her pet French Bulldog to the theatre every night and would put him down on the box office floor when we were signing the nightly financial statement.

"She's saying 'watch out for the dog' to my treasurers trying to do their job," I complained to the General Manager. "Why does the dog have to come to the box office every night?"

After a certain incident, to deescalate the tension between us, Peter Entin suggested I move over to the Cort Theatre for my last season since she and *Curious Dog* were due to stay at the Barrymore for another year at least.

I jokingly felt like I was being sent over to the dog's house. A new show was coming into the Cort called *Sylvia*, by A.R. "Pete" Gurney, which was about a family dog, to be played by the energetic, wonderful Annaleigh Ashford.

Matthew Broderick and Julie White were to play the husband and wife, the pet's owners. My old friends, Jeffrey Richards and

Daryl Roth, were the producers. I agreed, and a switch of managers was arranged.

The old Cort Theatre, built in 1912, was in sorry shape indeed. Joe Traina, my friend, when he was the manager of the Cort used to say: "When the Titanic was going down in 1912, this theatre was going up."

At this point, the ship at the bottom of the sea might have been in better shape. There was major construction on the block—once one of the great blocks in New York—with the many music stores lining 48th Street between 6th and 7th Avenues now closed down.

I was on the wrong side of Broadway again, but I was still happy. I painted the office and went to work.

The reviews for our revival were tepid at best. Though uniformly they praised Annaleigh and Julie White, they found the direction by Daniel Sullivan bland. Still, the audience loved the cleverness of Gurney's play. The playwright and his wife, both wonderful people, were at the theatre more than not. We limped into the end of the run through December and closed the first week in January, three weeks early.

I took a couple of my cousins from Bayville on Long Island backstage. The cast was most gracious and came onto the stage to greet them. First Annaleigh, and then Matthew Broderick. My cousin Douglas said, "Boy, I really loved your movie, *Glory*. What a great film."

"Thank you," Matthew said.

Then Douglas asked, "How come they never made a sequel?"

Matthew thought for a long second and said: "Well, because all the characters were dead in the end."

***

After a month, another attraction booked the Cort Theatre: *Bright Star*, a musical featuring the bluegrass music of the iconic comedian Steve Martin and Edie Brickell.

Early in the process, with the show just loading in, I was met at the back of the orchestra by Peter Entin who said he now wanted me to move over to the Longacre where they had *Allegiance,* a musical about the internment of Japanese-Americans during World War II with George Takei, Mr. Sulu from *Star Trek*. It was an odd request since I had just settled into the Cort Theatre and believed I would stay there for the season. But, whatever. I just wanted to put my time in and the Longacre, in fairness, was a beautiful theatre, having just been renovated a few years before, getting its very own water heater.

In mid-February the show was limping along, but not disastrously. Lorenzo Thione, who had become a tech multi-millionaire in Silicon Valley, was the producer. He had a part in writing the book of the show. Thione was happy to cover the losses through the Tony Awards in June, but it was not to be.

The theatre had been leased to a new show called *Nerds,* which was about the early lives of Bill Gates and Steve Jobs, and the development of the computer. Carl Levin, who had been one of the producers of *Rock of Ages*, was behind the wheel with this production. *Rock of Ages* had been a fun but boisterous production, with drinking and dancing allowed throughout the performance. Many a group of large partiers took it a bit too far, and the police were often called to maintain order.

We had taken *Allegiance* out of the theatre after its abrupt closing. We were loading in scenery for *Nerds* when Peter Entin came into the theatre and told us to load everything back out. Levin had a backer pull $5 million out of the production and he did not have the money to open, so a final dress rehearsal in a local studio was the end of *Nerds*, sadly.

I made it known at this point that I still had signed the contract at the Cort Theatre, which had a running show in it, namely *Bright Star*. According to union rules, I had to return to that job or be paid off. Mr. Entin decided to send me to the Golden Theatre where *Eclipsed* was playing.

This play was about women stolen during the Liberian Civil War in 2003 in Africa, one of whom has been taken as a wife by a warlord. It starred Lupita Nyong'o, a fast-rising movie star after her performance in the movie *Twelve Years a Slave*. It was written by Danai Gurira.

It might have done much better at the box office had Lupita not taken so many shows off. When that happens, the audience starts to figure the star won't be there the night they go, and ticket sales plummet.

There were many post-play discussions about the wars in Africa. The most moving involved a young woman, maybe twenty years old, who had been stolen from her school in Chubik, Nigeria, by the violent group, Boka Haram. She was forced to be the wife of an AK-47-carrying member. She had escaped her captors, and here she was on the stage of the Golden Theatre telling her moving story. It was amazing to think this brave young girl had been a prisoner less than a year before.

On July 19, the show closed as it was scheduled to. It had been a strange season indeed for me, and it was coming to an end. After the take-out was done, when the ghost light was placed center stage, I walked down the street to our Security Office on that hot July day and turned in the keys to the Golden Theatre.

My thirty-seven years working on Broadway were over.

What Will Happen?

As of this writing, a pandemic has closed all the theatres on Broadway, Off-Broadway, and everywhere else. Actors, writers, musicians, wardrobe people, stagehands, and all sit idly waiting for the day the marquees of Broadway glow again.

Will the great surge of tourism return? When will people feel comfortable sitting with a thousand other people in a darkened auditorium? Will the economics of Broadway work, with houses 80, 70, 60 percent full? Will the stagehands, Equity, the musicians of 802, and the other unions relent and take cuts to their deals?

Broadway is as vital to the great City of New York as Wall Street, the Garment District, the great museums, as anything. But the future is unknown.

On Opening Night, most musicals honor an old ceremony. A member of the chorus is awarded "the gypsy robe." A robe that is adorned with the emblems of other shows, from the dancers who have worn it on other Opening Nights. A ceremony that is a prayer more than anything else.

A prayer for health, for a good run, for joy in the playing.

What can one now say at this time but "Amen."

***

That prayer was written two years ago when the pandemic of COVID-19 was raging in America and around the world. A million Americans would die from it and it would keep the lights of Broadway dark for over two years.

I knew Jeremy Stole, who was playing Raul in *Phantom of the Opera,* but found himself unemployed. He had to paint apartments in New Jersey to survive with his wife and two children.

That is only one of thousands of stories of the Broadway people who had to take any job they could find to survive. Some gave up altogether and left the City, returning to the hometowns they originally came from.

Then the vaccines started to work, and the number of people ill slowly diminished. Broadway began to emerge from the dark clouds of the pandemic. Then a miracle happened. Broadway roared back to life with multiple productions funded by new producers whose participation often was simply signing a check. As always, the attrition rate is great. Only one in five Broadway shows truly "makes" it: returning the capital investment plus a dollar, the longtime definition of a hit.

Still, the investment money keeps flowing in, fueled by the fortunes made on Wall Street and in real estate over the last two decades.

Some shows like *Chicago* and *Wicked* keep running and running and they are joined by new hits like *Hadestown* and *Come From Away*.

Broadway, once called the "fabulous invalid," is back with its lights glowing and its theatres filled. Tourism has returned and Times Square is once again hard to walk around during the holidays. The fervent prayers of only a couple of years before have been answered.

Epilogue
The Final Bow

WHEN I LOOK BACK on the span of my years on Broadway, I remember things—images and feelings and people—in a hundred ways.

Leaving the theatre at night after the show and walking through crowds of people energized by the plays and musicals they had just seen.

The thrill of the first day of take-in, a new show, the loading doors opened for scenery and two hundred lights.

The long Saturday nights at the end of load-in week, finishing stagehand payrolls for thousands and thousands of dollars, trying to get it right to the penny, in an empty theatre where only I remained. I would always look at the stage before I left for the night, perhaps remembering my early days as an actor, full of dreams about being up there, just like the time I took Denzel Washington around the theatre and he stood on stage and looked out dreaming of a full house applauding at the curtain.

The night of the first preview, everyone there, the producers, the managers, all wanting to see what we had when the lights came up.

Opening night, the famous and rich of the world there to be seen as much as to see. The party afterward, fun and glittery, often ending early when the reviews came in. Buoyant and wild if the critics thought the show was wonderful.

Then afterward, driving to a late newsstand to pick up a copy of the papers to read the reviews for myself. Calling in the morning to ask the treasurers, "How long is the line to buy tickets?" Or if there was any line at all.

When I think back, what I remember first and foremost are the beautiful buildings, the theatres I worked in, and I worked in them all. The lath and plaster walls that can carry the sound of a finger snap to the back of the balcony. The character of design inside and out.

I remember the old Belasco, before its renovation in 2011, which rendered it as beautiful as it had ever been.

But before, there was a haunted feeling there. The stairs that lead to the manager's office went up into darkness all the way to David Belasco's apartment. Chilling.

Most Belasco Theatre ghost stories are of an old lady dressed in white sitting in the balcony, or being chased from room to room in the labyrinth of the backstage basement by Shubert Security, who saw her but could never find her. And lastly the tale of a porter who in mid-afternoon saw a bucket he had left with a mop in it, the mop spinning round and round by itself. He never came back to work, and no one blamed him.

The great large theatres. Like the Winter Garden, where a hole was created in the ceiling so Grisabella could ascend to heaven in

Cats. The Majestic where I did almost a year on *42nd Street*, and later *Phantom of the Opera.* The Imperial, home of *Les Misérables.* The old Shubert, where I first worked for Alex Cohen in his offices on top of the theatre, where Johnny Dollar would take me up in "his" elevator.

The smaller theatres I truly loved. The Broadhurst, my first. The Lyceum with memories of Whoopi. The Longacre, the theatre of the empty helmets. The Golden, the little jewel box. The Booth, where once John Cleese came up to me and asked where the hearing headsets were, claiming to have become a little deaf. I, ever the wise guy, said, "Oh, too many swords clanging on helmets?" referring to his Monty Python days.

The Jacobs and the Schoenfeld, with memories of *Once, Song and Dance, The Real Thing, Lend Me a Tenor.*

The odd Ambassador, a circular theatre on 48th Street, with a broom closet for the manager's office.

The beautiful Music Box, where my uncles Dan and Don played the choir boys in *The Man Who Came to Dinner*, thereby pulling my family out of the extreme poverty they knew throughout the 1930s.

The old Cort on 48th Street, once the street of music stores, one of which I visited to buy a Les Paul guitar for Christmas for my nephew Joshua after the death of his father, my brother, Chris.

And finally, the beautiful Barrymore, with all those stories of Tennessee and Marlon Brando, the Dames Maggie and Judi.

Yes, Michelle Pfeiffer, you call her Dame Judi.

Alec Baldwin, the great mimic, and Jessica Lange, at peace, sitting on the fire escape and puffing on a cigarette after the show.

The gentleman and lady producers, more kind to me than not. Those incredible moments of theatre, so unforgettable. The end of *A Chorus Line*, the eight remaining dancers all but broken, yet victorious, having won the job, which is what the theatre and show business are all about, anyway.

All of *Phantom, Les Mis*, and *Evita* with Patti LuPone belting it out to the heavens, or way up to the back balcony of the Broadway Theatre, much the same.

Coleen Dewhurst and Jason Robards, husband and wife, in *Moon for the Misbegotten*. Cherry Jones in *The Heiress*, and then again in *Doubt*, in the last seconds reaching to the sky seeking some sign of divinity and justice, the reason for her faith.

Ian McKellen, at the end of *Amadeus*, a senile, shaking old man, as his rival Mozart's genius soared through the world, while his music faded to vapor, finally saying, "Mediocrity is everywhere. I absolve you all. Amen." Along with a thousand other moments, all beautiful.

If we are allowed to dream for a minute or an hour after we pass, I suppose I would haunt the Barrymore at the back of the house, on the orchestra floor, where the staircase leads to the lower lounge, and up to the mezzanine. I would look through the curtain at the end of the show, as I often did, and Raul Esparza would be singing "Being Alive" from *Company* with Sondheim sitting in the back row. Then I would, as they say, move on.

In my career, I was not that important. I did not create the art as a player or writer, but I am proud of being who I was, and it was important enough. I was there for those moments. That's enough.

I have no advice to give, save this. I was called to an audition in the 1970s when I was still a young actor. It was at the Manhattan Theatre Club when it was up on 73rd Street. I waited in a large room by myself until I was called in to do my audition. I went over my lines that I had been given "on sides," as all actors do.

An old woman came into the hall, obviously to audition for the same play. It was paying $300 a week. I looked up from my script, then again. There was something very familiar about this simply dressed woman. Then I realized who she was.

It was Margaret Hamilton, who had played the Wicked Witch of the West in *The Wizard of Oz* with Judy Garland. In her day, one of the most famous actresses in the world.

I was called to come into the room for my audition. I got up and walked past her. My eyes met hers. I nodded to say I know who you are, and good luck. I did not get the part, and I don't know if she got hers, and this is the lesson.

Simply put, the problem with a life in show business is not that it is short. The problem is that it is long, as we ever try for another moment in the lights, or that time of simply being there, part of it all, until the stage glow fades, the story told.

About the Author

DAN LANDON began his career in New York as an actor, appearing on Broadway (for one opening night) and Off-Broadway. He then turned to theatre management, first at the American Place Theatre, then for legendary producer Alex Cohen, and then for three decades with the Shuberts. Dan is also a produced playwright and published novelist. His plays have appeared Off-Broadway and regionally. He lived for many years in Montclair, New Jersey, with his wife, Lyle, and their three children. After his retirement, they moved to Bradenton, Florida, where both he and Lyle are active in the theatre scene on the Gulf Coast.

DAN LANDON
Theatre Manager Extraordinaire

A gift from my wife, Lyle,
commemorating my 28 years at the Barrymore Theatre.

Also By Dan Landon

PLAYS

Punchy

The Night the Lights Went Out

Two Detectives

Gatsby: A New American musical

Happy Dale

Basic Training (one-act)

The Dry, Dry Dessert of the Mind (one-act)

NOVELS

Lefty: How Dutch Schultz tried to fix 1932 World Series

Stories Take Flight at Ibis Books

The IBIS is sacred to Thoth,
the Egyptian god of learning,
inventor of writing,
and scribe to the gods.

They are gregarious birds that live,
travel, and breed in flocks.

And they are legendary for their courage.

ibisbooks.shop

Printed in Great Britain
by Amazon

44955306R00148